ENERGY

WHAT EVERYONE NEEDS TO KNOW

ENERGY
WHAT EVERYONE NEEDS TO KNOW

JOSÉ GOLDEMBERG

OXFORD
UNIVERSITY PRESS

OXFORD
UNIVERSITY PRESS

Oxford University Press, Inc., publishes works that further
Oxford University's objective of excellence
in research, scholarship, and education.

Oxford   New York
Auckland   Cape Town   Dar es Salaam   Hong Kong   Karachi
Kuala Lumpur   Madrid   Melbourne   Mexico City   Nairobi
New Delhi   Shanghai   Taipei   Toronto

With offices in
Argentina   Austria   Brazil   Chile   Czech Republic   France   Greece
Guatemala   Hungary   Italy   Japan   Poland   Portugal   Singapore
South Korea   Switzerland   Thailand   Turkey   Ukraine   Vietnam

Published by Oxford University Press, Inc.
198 Madison Avenue, New York, New York 10016

www.oup.com

Oxford is a registered trademark of Oxford University Press

Library of Congress Cataloging-in-Publication Data
Goldemberg, José, 1928–
Energy : what everyone needs to know / José Goldemberg.
p.   cm.
Includes bibliographical references and index.
ISBN 978-0-19-981292-9 (pbk. : alk. paper)
ISBN 978-0-19-981290-5 (hardcover : alk. paper)
1. Energy conservation.   2. Energy consumption.
3. Energy development.   4. Energy industries.   5. Power resources.
I. Title.
TJ163.3.G65 2012
333.79—dc23   2011044525

1 3 5 7 9 8 6 4 2

Printed in the United States of America
on acid-free paper

CONTENTS

PART II THE WORLD'S PRESENT ENERGY SYSTEM

PART IV TECHNICAL SOLUTIONS AND POLICIES

10 Energy Efficiency 105

11 New Technologies 119

LIST OF TABLES

LIST OF FIGURES

PREFACE

Energy is an essential ingredient of life. Without energy there is no movement, no moving machinery, no telecommunication— no human life. At the dawn of civilization, energy needs were very modest; humans only needed enough energy, which was obtained through the food they collected and ate, to remain alive. The amount of energy that one human needed per day at this time equaled the amount contained in a cup of petroleum. Today, each of us needs at least one hundred times more energy per day, which, worldwide, means billions of barrels of oil and coal per year to run our automobiles and trucks, and coal, hydroelectricity, and nuclear reactors to generate electricity. Without energy our civilization would come to a halt. The problem is that in the 21st century almost all of the energy we use originates in fossil fuels (coal, petroleum, and gas). Such dependence creates serious problems that threaten our way of life: it exhausts the reserves of fossil fuels and results in environmental problems, particularly the warming of the Earth. In order to face such problems and do something about them, one should know more about energy. We will try to do that by answering a number of leading questions organized into five sections:

HOW IS ENERGY USED TODAY? What are the human needs for energy, and how do they relate to economic growth and other indicators of well-being?

THE WORLD'S PRESENT ENERGY SYSTEM: What are the current primary sources of energy and how are they used?

THE PROBLEMS OF THE PRESENT ENERGY SYSTEM: What are the problems faced by the present energy system?

TECHNICAL SOLUTIONS AND POLICIES: What are the technical solutions to present energy problems and what policies could bring them about?

NONTECHNICAL SOLUTIONS: Are there nontechnical solutions to the present energy problems?

Before doing that, in a chapter entitled *ENERGY—The basic concepts* we will summarize some ideas that will be useful in understanding subjects that appear later in the book.

ENERGY

WHAT EVERYONE NEEDS TO KNOW

1

ENERGY

The Basic Concepts

What are forces?

In order to live and move around, human beings need to overcome gravity, or the force of attraction that the Earth exerts on all objects. They must also overcome other obstacles to movement, such as friction. With muscular effort, humans manage to overcome such obstacles and thus lift bodies or set them into motion. There are a variety of forces in nature, aside from the force of our muscles.

Isaac Newton (1642–1727) named force any agent capable of causing bodies to move. He established a relation that determines the amount of force necessary to cause a certain movement:

$$\text{force (F)} = \text{mass (m)} \times \text{acceleration (a)}.$$

Forces are measured in newtons (N). The gravitational force on 1 kilogram (kg) of matter is 9.8 N.

Frequently, it is not enough to apply a force to a body to make it move. For example, the horses that pull a wagon must also overcome the friction that exists between the wagon and the road.

What is work?

When an object falls from a given height above the surface of the Earth, the force of gravity (F) results in a quantity of work

(W) defined as the product of the force and the distance the object travels (d):

work (W) = force (F) × distance (d).

The unit commonly used for work is the joule (J), which is the energy needed to lift a small 102-gram (g) apple 1 meter (m) against the Earth's gravity.

What is energy?

If one wanted to lift the same object to the height from which it originally fell, the person would need to spend a given amount of energy exactly equal to W. Energy may be defined as the capacity to produce work.

The energy may be kinetic (for example, the force deriving from waves and winds), gravitational (from waterfalls), electric (from turbines and batteries), chemical (obtained from exothermic reactions, such as diesel and gasoline combustion), thermal (from burning charcoal or wood), radiant (from sunlight), and nuclear (obtained from the fission of uranium atoms or the fusion of hydrogen nuclei). Some forms are more useful than others; several can be transformed. For example, the energy obtained from a nuclear reaction may be used to heat water and produce high pressure steam, which, in turn, can produce work to move a turbine to produce electricity.

The ability to move objects is essential to our survival, and the amount of work needed for that depends very much on how much we do and the energy we expend.

Which are the common forces in nature?

There are three types of forces that are considered fundamental: gravitational, electromagnetic, and nuclear.

Gravitational forces exist between bodies, owing to their mass. It is part of our everyday experience that all bodies fall downward when set free. Since ancient times, scientists have studied the movement of bodies when falling, but Isaac Newton, who studied gravitational forces in 17th-century England, was the first to fully understand them. What Newton did was to realize that one could understand why bodies fall to the ground, why the Moon rotates around the Earth, and why the Earth circles around the Sun. He introduced the idea that there is an attractive force between any two bodies, with masses m_1 and m_2, and that the force is proportional to the mass of these bodies; this force decreases as the distance between them increases, proportionally to the inverse square of the distance. This is the Law of Universal Gravitation. It is possible to show that all the Earth exerts an attraction on a body as if its whole mass were concentrated at its center. *Electromagnetic* (electric and magnetic) forces exist due to electric charges. Electric forces are attractive when they have different charges (positive and negative) or repulsive when having the same charge. Magnetism has been understood since the 5th century before the Christian era. The Greeks were familiar with the attractive (and repulsive) forces that existed between certain minerals, which the Chinese used to build compasses as an aid to navigation. The Greeks noted, too, that amber, when rubbed against furs, acquired the ability to attract small objects. By the 17th century, scientists understood that materials rubbed against furs took on attractive as well as repulsive forces. This understanding gave rise to the idea, introduced by Benjamin Franklin in 1747, of positive and negative "electricity." Franklin also clarified that lightning is caused by "electricity" accumulated in clouds.

In 1785 Charles-Augustin de Coulomb began to measure these forces. What he found was that the law of attraction (or repulsion) between two charges is similar to the gravitational attraction existing between two bodies: it is proportional to the amount of electricity in the two bodies and inversely proportional to the square of the distance between them.

Heinrich Hertz discovered that rapidly oscillating electric charges generate electromagnetic waves that propagate in space and have an electric and a magnetic component. His discovery opened the way to radio communication, and later to television.

Nuclear forces exist among the constituents of the nucleus of the atoms.

The basic constituents of matter are atoms, which have a structure similar to that of solar system, in which planets turn around a central body (as the Earth circles the Sun). In atoms, electrons (which have negative charges) are attracted and move around the nucleus of the atom (which contains the positively charged protons) the same way as planets circle around the Sun. As a whole, atoms are electrically neutral. Typically atoms are 10^{-8} cm in diameter. Molecules are made up by a combination of atoms.

The chemical elements are characterized according to the number of electrons each has circling its nucleus: for example, hydrogen has 1 electron, helium 2, and uranium 92. The nucleus has very small dimensions, typically 10^{-13} cm in diameter. Therefore, the repulsion among the protons is very strong. To counteract these forces, there are nuclear forces that bind the protons together when they are separated by distances smaller than 10^{-13} cm. In the nucleus there are also particles that have no charge (called neutrons) that have a role in this binding process.

The expansive force of gases has also been known since antiquity, but the study of the expansive force developed completely independent of the study of mechanics. The two studies were unified at the end of the 18th century when scientists realized that mechanical work can be transformed entirely into heat. J. J. Thomson (1753–1814) first noted this when observing the process of boring holes into iron blocks used to manufacture cannons. In 1843 James Prescott Joule established the mechanical equivalent of heat.

More recently, the kinetic theory of gases led to a full understanding of the intimate connection between mechanical work and heat. According to this theory, gases are formed when molecules collide with each other and with the walls of the object holding them. Heat, therefore, is nothing other than mechanical energy: the higher the temperature, the higher the average velocity of the molecules.

What is friction?

Friction is not a fundamental force like gravitational or electromagnetic forces. It originates in surface irregularities and/or forces between objects that come into contact with each other. Its characteristics are entirely empiric and depend on the nature of the surfaces in contact.

For example, two very clean glass plates, once put into contact, even in a vacuum, will be difficult to separate. It is as if there were "tentacles" that, starting from one surface, retain the other, making it necessary to break them to separate them.

Friction has a very important role in the performance of all kinds of machines, because overcoming it requires work that otherwise would be used for other purposes. Friction is thus sometimes referred to as a "dissipative force," which is irreversible. If the movement is reversed, such as in the sliding of two surfaces against each other, energy would have to be spent again.

In the absence of friction, the continuous movement of a system that periodically returns to its original position, such as an oscillating pendulum, would be possible. But in reality air causes friction, so the amplitude of an oscillation is reduced gradually until it stops. In a vacuum a pendulum would oscillate much longer before slowing down and stopping, since the only existing friction is at the point of suspension.

How does one measure energy?

One joule is defined as the work performed by a force of 1 newton (N) in a displacement of 1 m. The force of gravity on 1 kg of matter is 9.8 N; therefore, 1 J is the amount of energy needed to lift a body of 102 g to a height of 1 m.

That amount of work (or the energy needed to produce it) can also be measured in calories. One calorie is the quantity of energy needed to increase the temperature of 1 g of water by 1°C (e.g., from 13.5 °C to 14.5 °C). One calorie is equivalent to 4.18 J.

The time necessary to perform a given amount of work is of great importance. For example, a man can lift 40 25-kg stones, one by one, from the ground and place them into a cart. But he will be unable to lift all of them (1,000 kg) in a single operation, despite the total work done in the two cases being exactly the same. The amount of work performed per unit of time is called power (P), and it is measured in watts (W). One watt is equal to 1 joule per second (J/s). The unit employed to measure power in many countries is the "horsepower" (or HP, equivalent to about 746 W), which traditionally represented the "power" of a horse or 7.5 times the power of a man.

The human being, on average, consumes energy at a power of about 100 W (the power of an average incandescent light bulb), varying between 85 W during sleep and 800 W or more during intense exercises.

Table 1.1 Units of work, energy, and power

1 joule (J)	=	10^7 ergs
1 watt (W)	=	1 J/s
1 HP	=	746 W
1 cal	=	4.18 J
1 kilowatt-hour (kWh)	=	3.6×10^{13} ergs = 3,600 kj
		860 kcal = 8.6×10^{15} toe
1 toe (ton of oil equivalent)	=	$10,000 \times 10^3$ kcal
	=	1.28 ton of coal
	=	11,630 kWh
1 BTU (British thermal unit)	=	252 cal
1 kW-year/year	=	0.753 toe/year

A unit used frequently is the ton of oil equivalent (toe), which is equal to 10 million kcal (10^{10} cal), since 1 kg of oil contains 10,000 kcal. It is usual to convert the energy of all other sources of energy to tons of oil equivalent, including electrical energy, measured in kilowatt-hours.

Table 1.1 lists the commonly used units.

Can energy be created from nothing?

As man developed tools, such as axles or levers, to make his work easier, a great effort was made to find machines that could perform work without the need of muscular effort. The human spirit has always been fascinated by the idea of building a "perpetuum mobile" or perpetual motion machine, which, once set in motion, would never stop. All the efforts to build such machines failed. The reason for such failures is the nature of Newton's law of gravitational force; energy performed involving the force of gravity is always conserved, that is, remains constant and cannot be created or destroyed. For example, if a body falls from a given height, a given and constant amount of work is performed. To lift the body to the same height requires exactly the same amount of work as is performed when the object falls, independent of the trajectory one follows in order to lift the object.

This is a most fundamental discovery because it means that energy cannot be created or destroyed. The consequence is that it is impossible to construct a machine in the gravitational field that produces mechanical work, such as grinding cereals, without the addition of a source of energy from outside the system.

Robert Fludd made one of the most interesting proposals for a "perpetuum mobile" machine in 1630 (Figure 1.1). He designed a machine in which the force of gravity would move a waterwheel connected to an endless bolt, which would, in turn, move all the water back to the original reservoir; the

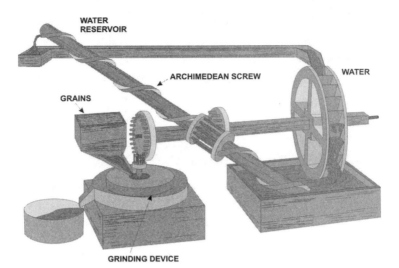

Figure 1.1 Fludd's "perpetuum mobile" machine

turning of the water wheel would drive a device to grind corn or other cereals.

Obviously this contraption didn't work.

What is the First Law of Thermodynamics?

The law of conservation of mechanical energy can be extended to include thermal phenomena. In an isolated system the sum of the mechanical and thermal energies is conserved. This is the First Law of Thermodynamics, which states that the total variation of energy contained in a closed system is equal to the (net) effect of the heat and work the system undergoes with the environment. In other words, energy can neither be created nor destroyed, an example of which is work performed by gravitational forces.

The First Law can be extended to include all forms of energy: mechanical, thermal, electrical, magnetic, chemical, and nuclear.

PART I

HOW IS ENERGY USED TODAY?

2

PRESENT ENERGY USE

How much energy do humans need to keep alive?

The daily minimum energy an adult human needs to live is approximately 1,000 kilocalories (1 million calories). A person who consumes less than this amount of energy will lose weight and may eventually die. World War II prisoners in concentration camps received less than 1,000 kcal/day. An adult engaged in normal activities needs about 2,000 kcal/day, which is the amount of energy contained in a cup of petroleum. For a person performing heavy manual work, 4,000 kcal/day are necessary. Table 2.1 shows the energy needs for a number of human tasks.

How much energy do humans need for other activities?

To satisfy the growing needs of human beings in modern societies, a considerable increase in energy consumption is necessary.

Looking through history, one can clearly see that, as human beings have advanced technologically, their energy needs have also increased. Figure 2.1 shows the relationship between human development and energy needs across four categories: food, home and commerce, industry and agriculture, and transportation.

Table 2.1 Energy needs for different activities

Effort	Example	Energy consumption (kcal/hour)
	light activities	50–60
Light to moderate	walk	125–180
	light work (e.g., carpentry)	150–180
	march	280
	break stones	350
Heavy	row, swim, run	400–700
	intensive sports	800–1,000

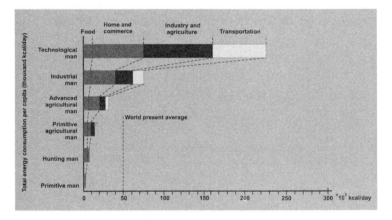

Figure 2.1 Stages of development and energy consumption per capita

A million years ago, primitive man from Eastern Africa had not yet mastered fire and relied only on the energy from food ingested (some 2,000 kcal/day). A hundred thousand years ago, hunting man already consumed more food and burned wood to cook and heat his hut. Later, primitive agricultural man from Mesopotamia (10,000 BCE) used the energy of working animals for agricultural activities. In the early Modern Ages (1,400 CE), advanced agricultural man from Northeastern Europe used coal for heating and the mechanical energy from waterfalls and wind. During this period, transportation also became an important role in commerce. In England, in 1875, industrial man developed the steam engine, and commerce and transportation increased substantially. Later, in the 20th century, technological man improved the steam engine and developed internal combustion engines (Otto and Diesel cycles), electric engines, and nuclear energy. Consumption per capita in industrialized countries reached more than 100 times the consumption of primitive man.

Presently the world's average energy consumption is approximately 1.8 toe per year (50,000 kcal/day). Energy consumption in the United States is approximately six times higher (300,000 kcal/day) than the world average.

What are the sources of energy we use?

Until the late Middle Ages the main source of energy used by the human population originated in biomass, or renewable and biologically based energy sources, namely, agriculture and forestry. As a consequence, a large share of the European forests was cut down for this fuel. However, with the growing population and consumption of energy, humans explored new sources of primary energy besides fuel wood, such as the rivers, which could supply hydraulic energy; coal for heating and generating steam; oil and products derived from it by distillation (gasoline, diesel, oil, and fuel oil) for moving internal combustion engines; and uranium for generating thermonuclear power.

Figure 2.2 charts the enormous growth in the consumption of energy since the beginning of the 20th century, as machines and new technology came into use. It also shows the gradual increase of coal, oil, gas, nuclear, and renewable energies.

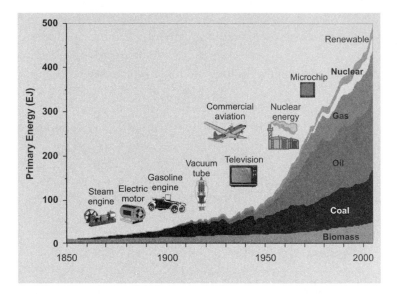

Figure 2.2 The sources of energy used since 1850

What is the origin of the energy we use?

The Earth is bombarded continuously by radiation from the Sun, with an intensity of 1,363 W/m² per year, which corresponds to 173,000,000 W incident on the whole Earth. Approximately 30% of this radiation is reflected into the atmosphere and reemitted back to space. The remaining 70% is responsible for producing the Earth's climate, and 23% of this radiation is consumed in evaporation of the water in the oceans, circulation of the water vapor, and water precipitation in what is called the hydrological cycle. A fraction of the water accumulates in lakes above sea level or in rivers, from where it runs back to the oceans. In the process it can generate hydroelectricity. The final 47% of the Sun's energy is absorbed by the atmosphere, warming the air, the oceans, and the surface of the Earth (determining its average temperature). The warming of the air gives rise to

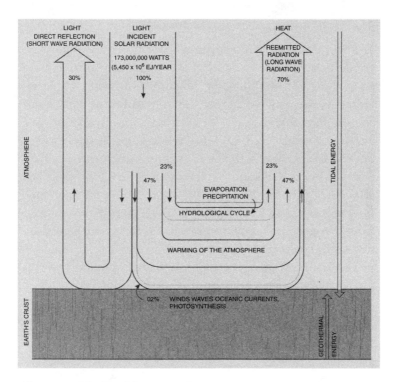

Figure 2.3 The Earth's energy flows

winds, which can be used to generate electricity in wind machines; wind also generates ocean waves. A small fraction of the incident solar radiation is captured by plants through photosynthesis, which allows them to form organic matter (e.g., fuel wood). Occasionally the remains of other organic matter (e.g., plankton and marine animals) accumulate or are buried through sedimentation or geological activity such as earthquakes. In these cases the lack of oxygen prevents complete combustion. Over millions of years, such buried organic matter is transformed into oil (petroleum), natural gas, and coal. These are the fossil fuels we are using today (Figure 2.3).

At what rate is energy consumption growing?

The world energy consumption grew by an average 2.2% annually between 1971 and 2006, which is approximately equivalent to a doubling of consumption every 30 years. However, growth is uneven among different sources of energy: annually, it is 1.8% for coal, 1.3% for oil, 2.0% for gas, 0.7% for nuclear, and 6.6% for renewables. It is also very uneven across nations. In developed countries growth is 1.4% per year, but in developing countries it is 3.2% each year. The total energy consumption in the Organization for Economic Cooperation and Development (OECD) countries stabilized from the year 2000 onward and was recently surpassed by non-OECD members.

The main drivers of energy growth are population growth and increased energy consumption "per capita."

What is the relationship between population growth and energy growth?

Population growth is one of the major determining factors in the increase in energy consumption. Between 1850 and 1990, the average annual population growth was 1.1% and the total energy consumption growth was 2.2%.

The evolution of population growth over the last 12,000 years is given in Table 2.2.

Projections indicate that the population of the world could reach 8.6 billion in the year 2050 and 10.2 billion in the year 2100. Because population growth is one of the main factors determining energy consumption in the next few decades, it is important to list the factors that could determine reductions in this growth. The main causes of population growth are unplanned pregnancies, desire for large family size, and population momentum (a consequence of people having children at a young age).

Table 2.2 Population and stages of development

Stage of development	Year	Population (millions)	Energy consumption/ capita/day ($\times 10^3$ kcal/ capita/day)
Primitive agricultural	10,000 BCE	80	12
	0 CE	300	
Advanced agriculture	1400 CE	500	20
Industrial man	1875 CE	1,400	77
Technological man	2000 CE	6,100	200

Reducing unwanted pregnancies by strengthening family planning programs could reduce the population from 10.2 to 8.3 billion by the year 2100. Reducing the demand for large families through investments in human development could lead to a further reduction from 8.3 to 7.3 billion in the year 2100.

The population momentum could be slowed if the average childbearing age of women was raised. By increasing the average age of childbearing by 5 years, we could achieve a further reduction from 7.3 to 6.1 billion by the year 2100. All such reductions are theoretical upper limits of what could be achieved, but they highlight the possible actions that could bring about a real reduction in population growth in the next century.

As is well known, the developed countries have experienced demographic transitions that have led to the total fertility rate (TFR) falling to approximately two, which is the replacement rate. The precise causes for the decline of TFR are very complex and synergetic in nature, including those listed above. The developing countries can be expected to follow a similar trend.

Why is energy consumption "per capita" growing?

The growth in energy consumption is linked to the development of cities; in the past, primitive agricultural societies used modest amounts of energy per capita for food, home, commerce, and industrial agriculture. Energy was mainly obtained through the use of domestic animals and slaves. As urban life developed, the increased demand for buildings and transportation required more energy. However, the "explosion" in energy growth per capita really began with the development of machines such as the steam engine, which opened the way for railroads and a great expansion in commerce and transportation—and the building of the great cities. The discovery of electricity at the end of the 19th century opened the way to modern technologies such as refrigerators, washing machines, radio, TV, and telecommunications, all of which revolutionized our consumption patterns and produced a corresponding increase in per capita consumption.

What is the relationship between energy and development?

Income growth is an aspiration of most people and is usually associated with development. A higher per capita income means that individuals can afford more material possessions—such as cars, domestic appliances, and better houses—all of which require more energy to build and use. However, the relationship between income per capita and energy consumption is a complex one.

Figure 2.4 plots the gross domestic product (GDP) per capita of a number of countries against commercial energy consumption per capita (in toe) per year. GDP is measured in power purchasing parity dollars of the year 2000.

Coal, oil, natural gas, and electricity are all commercial types of energy. Noncommercial energy or traditional energy includes locally collected and unprocessed biomass-based fuels such as crop residues, wood, and animal dung.

It is obviously a gross simplification to assume a linear relationship among these two indicators, although this is a concept that has been used repeatedly (and continues to be adopted) as a planning tool in many countries.

There are at least three reasons why energy consumption and income are not linked or linearly related.

We can first look at the historical evidence: in the United States between 1850 and 1950, or the initial phase of the industrialization in that country, energy consumption per capita grew more rapidly than income per capita. From 1950 on, the opposite happened, with income growing more rapidly than energy consumption. This occurred due to a shift from infrastructure building to services, which involve less intensive use of energy.

Second, we can compare industrialized countries: in the United States consumption per capita is 40% higher than in Sweden for the same income per capita despite the harsher climate. This is due basically to the fact that Sweden has better insulated homes and smaller and more efficient automobiles.

Finally, we can compare industrialized countries and developing countries: in developing countries—mostly located in the equatorial zone—the climate is milder and, consequently, less energy is needed for heating purposes. In addition, noncommercial sources of energy are important in developing countries, particularly in rural areas where the economy is based on a barter system and not measured in dollars—a fact that is not captured in graphs like the one shown in Figure 2.4.

What is energy intensity?

Energy intensity (I, as below) is defined as the ratio of energy to GDP:

$$I = E/GDP.$$

The evolution, over time, of the energy intensity of a country reflects combined effects of structural changes in the economy

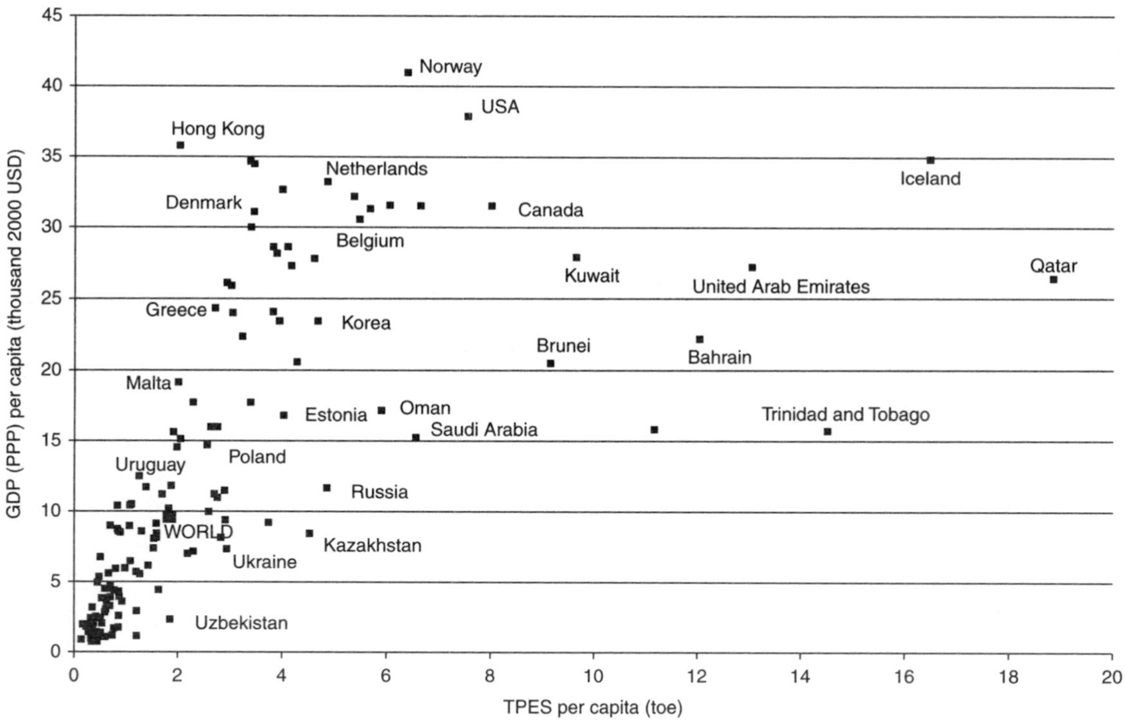

Figure 2.4 Relation between gross domestic product (GDP) per capita and per capita energy use (2008)

(built into the GDP) and changes in the mix of energy sources and the efficiency of energy use (built into the primary energy consumed, or E).

For some industrialized countries, such as the United Kingdom, United States, Germany, France, and Japan, data are available that permit tracking of the evolution of energy intensity over more than a century (Figure 2.5). Such tracking allows us to see that energy intensity increased as infrastructure and heavy industry developed, eventually reaching a peak and then steadily declining. Latecomers in the industrialization process, such as Japan, peaked at lower energy intensities than their predecessors, indicating early adoption of innovative and modern, energy-efficient industrial processes and technologies.

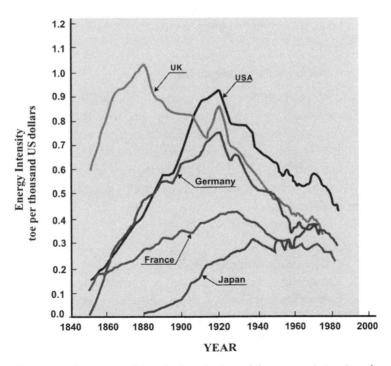

Figure 2.5 Long-term historical evolution of the energy intensity of industrialized countries

Although admittedly a very rough indicator, energy intensity has some attractive features: while E and GDP per capita vary by more than one order of magnitude between developing and developed countries, energy intensity does not change by more than a factor of 2. This is due in part to the fact that the energy systems of industrialized and developing countries in the "modern" sector of the economy have common characteristics.

Particularly after the oil crisis of the 1970s, industrialized countries successfully reduced their consumption of fossil fuels through improvements in the efficiency of energy use and the structural changes that led to post-industrial economies. As a result of a combination of these factors, the energy intensity of OECD countries has been falling by about 2.3% a year during the past few decades, although it is still growing in many developing countries at a rate of approximately 1.2% per year.

What is the Human Development Index?

In addition to income per capita there are a number of other indicators such as longevity, literacy, and total fertility rate that seem to be closely correlated with energy consumption. For that reason a more complex indicator, the Human Development Index (HDI), has been proposed to correct some of the shortcomings of the use of per capita income as a measure of development.

The HDI is a composite of:

- Longevity as measured by life expectancy;
- Knowledge, as measured by a combination of adult literacy (two-thirds weight) and mean years of schooling (one-third weight); and
- Standard of living, as measured by purchasing power, based on real GDP per capita adjusted for the local cost of living (or purchasing parity power—PPP).

Each of these indicators is given a value between 0 and 1 and the resulting numbers averaged in an overall index. For example, if the minimum for life expectancy is 25 years and the maximum is 85 years, the longevity component for a country where life expectancy is 55 years would be 0.5. A similar procedure is used for knowledge and standard of living.

Figure 2.6 plots HDI as a function of per capita commercial energy consumption per year for a large number of countries.

It is apparent from Figure 2.6 that, for an energy consumption above 2 toe per capita per year, the value of HDI is higher than 0.8 and essentially constant for all countries. That amount of energy per capita, therefore, seems to be the minimum energy needed to guarantee an acceptable level of living as measured by the HDI, despite many variations of consumption patterns and lifestyles across countries. A similar HDI for countries with different incomes per capita means that a lower income is compensated by a greater longevity and increased knowledge.

As can also be seen from Figure 2.6, a significant part of the world population in many countries has a very low HDI. Analysis conducted by the World Bank has indicated that there are more than 2 billion people without access to adequate energy services based on the use of gaseous and liquid fuels, as well as electricity. Without access to energy, opportunities for economic development and improved living standards are constrained. Women and children suffer disproportionately.

Access to affordable energy services is fundamental to human activities, development, and economic growth. Wide disparities in access to affordable commercial energy and energy services in both urban centers and rural areas are inequitable, run counter to the concept of human development, and threaten social stability.

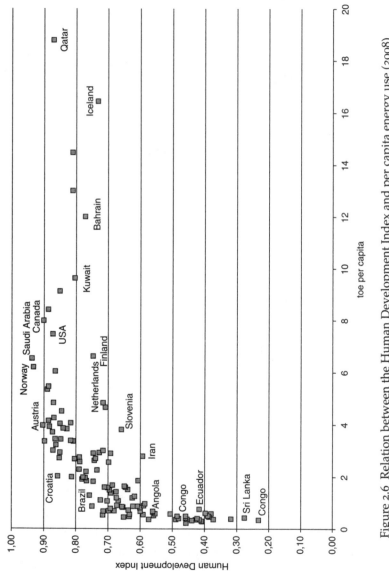

Figure 2.6 Relation between the Human Development Index and per capita energy use (2008)

What is the Gross National Happiness Index?

The concept of gross national happiness (GNH) was developed in an attempt to define an indicator that measures quality of life or social progress in broader terms than GDP or HDI, including measurements of well-being and happiness.

In one of its variants, the GNH is the average of indicators derived from statistical data such as economic wellness, environmental wellness, physical wellness, mental wellness, workplace wellness, social wellness, political wellness, consumer debt, pollution levels, income distribution, illnesses, use of antidepressants, jobless claims, rates of diversity, crime rates, and individual freedom.

Global surveys of GNH have been made for many countries, but they have received wide criticism because GNH depends on subjective judgments about the real meaning of well-being.

PART II

THE WORLD'S PRESENT ENERGY SYSTEM

3

ENERGY SOURCES

Which are the primary energy sources?

The world's energy system is very large: in 2008 it amounted to 492 exajoules, corresponding to 11.75 billion tons of oil equivalent (toe). With a population of almost 6.7 billion people, this corresponds approximately to 1.75 toe per capita per year (Figure 3.1).

The primary energy sources are:

- Solar, responsible for hydropower, wind, photovoltaic, and solar thermal energy as well as the production of biomass and, ultimately, the fossil fuels (coal, oil, and gas);
- Geothermal energy, originating in the molten core of the Earth;
- Tidal energy, originating in the gravitational attraction from the Moon; and
- Nuclear energy, originating in the nuclei of atoms.

Renewable energy sources are the ones produced from geo-physical or biological sources that are naturally replenished at the rate of extraction. Biomass, hydropower, wind energy, photovoltaic solar energy, high-temperature solar thermal energy, low-temperature solar energy, geothermal, and ocean

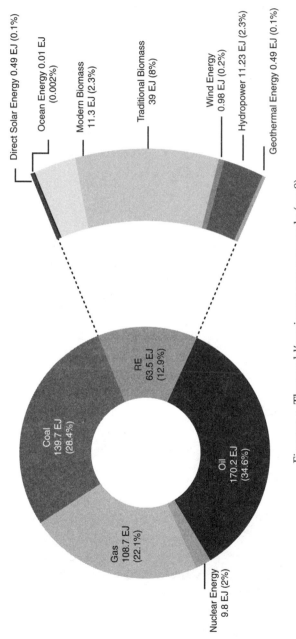

Direct Solar Energy 0.49 EJ (0.1%)

Ocean Energy 0.01 EJ (0.002%)

Modern Biomass 11.3 EJ (2.3%)

Traditional Biomass 39 EJ (8%)

Wind Energy 0.98 EJ (0.2%)

Hydropower 11.23 EJ (2.3%)

Geothermal Energy 0.49 EJ (0.1%)

Coal 139.7 EJ (28.4%)

RE 63.5 EJ (12.9%)

Oil 170.2 EJ (34.6%)

Gas 108.7 EJ (22.1%)

Nuclear Energy 9.8 EJ (2%)

Figure 3.1 The world's primary energy supply (2008)

Table 3.1 The main sources of energy

Source of energy	Energy (watts)
Solar	173,000,000
Geothermal	32
Gravitational (tides)	3

energy in the form of waves and tides are all renewable. Nuclear power is not strictly renewable because uranium reserves (from which nuclear power is produced) are finite, although they can last for a long time at the present rate of consumption.

Sun's energy is, by far, the dominant source of energy on Earth (Table 3.1).

The world's energy matrix in 2008 was dominated by fossil fuels, of which oil composed 34.6% of the total, coal 28.4%, natural gas 22.1%, and nuclear 2.0% representing

Table 3.2 The world's primary energy sources (2008)

Energy source	EJ	%	Gtoe[a]
Coal	139.7	28.4	3.34
Oil	170.2	34.6	4.06
Gas	108.7	22.1	2.59
Nuclear	9.8	2	0.23
Hydropower	11.23	2.3	0.27
Traditional biomass	39	8	0.93
Modern biomass	11.3	2.3	0.27
Wind	0.98	0.2	0.02
Geothermal	0.49	0.1	0.01
Direct solar energy	0.49		0.01
Ocean energy	0.01	0.002	–
Total	492.00	100.0	11.75

[a] 1 Gtoe = 41.87 EJ

87.1% of the total. Renewable energies represented the remaining 12.9% and can be broken down into traditional biomass (8%), modern biomass (2.3%), hydropower (2.3%), wind energy (0.2%), geothermal (0.1%), direct solar energy (0.1%), and ocean energy (0.002%). Modern biomass includes bioethanol, biodiesel, electricity, and CHP (combined heat and power).

The contribution of all primary energy sources is given in Table 3.2.

What are secondary energy sources?

The primary energy sources (oil, coal, gas, hydro, uranium, and renewables) must usually undergo significant transformations in order to be used. For example, there is a long way between the extraction of coal (which is a primary source of energy), to a power plant, which converts the coal into electricity (a secondary source of energy), and finally, distribution through the electricity grid for end uses such as light bulbs. Usually 30% of the primary energy is lost in the transformation to secondary energy.

The final uses of energy are usually classified as industry, transport, residential, commercial, and public services, and nonenergy uses, as indicated in Table 3.3.

Table 3.3 The world's final uses of energy—2008

Sector	Million toe	%
Industry	2,435	28.8
Transport	2,299	27.3
Residential	2,024	24.0
Commercial and public services	0.693	8.2
Other (agric. forestry)	0.323	3.8
Nonenergy use	0.747	8.9
Total	8.428	100.0

Why are there losses in converting energy sources?

The most important transformations in the transition of primary energy sources to consumable end products are the production of electricity and motive power. This process is usually done by burning fossil fuels to produce steam, which then is used to produce mechanical power or electricity.

The idea of using vapor from boiling water to produce mechanical power has a long history. For example, the Greeks used the expansive force of gases to open the doors in temples without the intervention of human hands 2,500 years ago. This probably had an extraordinary impact on the Athenians.

However, to produce mechanical work in a sustained way, one needs a machine that will operate in a cycle, that is, will continually resume an initial operation and repeat it successively. To open the doors of temples does not meet that requirement. By the late 18th century, the English blacksmith and mechanic Thomas Newcomen (1663–1729) managed to do it, with a huge low-power machine (approximately 4 hp) that consumed coal at a high rate and an efficiency of less than 2%. This machine was originally used in coal mines to pump water. Newcomen's engine, besides being very big, needed a man to operate the valves. The cycles were spaced over time.

James Watt (1736–1839) improved the system in the early 19th century, thermally insulating the cylinder and introducing an external condenser that cooled the steam, feeding it back into the cylinder. The machine's efficiency increased to about 5%. As the machines continued to be improved and their efficiency increased, they were able to be operated far from the coal mines (Figure 3.2).

At a certain point, engineers introduced speed regulators into steam engines and the textile industry started to use them on a large scale. They were also used in railway engines, giving rise to the Industrial Revolution.

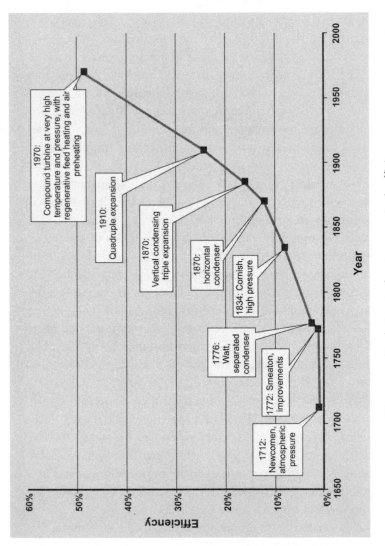

Figure 3.2 Evolution in the steam engine's efficiency

These improvements in steam engine efficiency led Sadi Carnot, as early as 1824, to investigate whether there was any theoretical limit to the efficiency of thermal machines, that is, in the conversion of the expansion of gases into mechanical work.

What Carnot demonstrated is that when transferring heat from a high-temperature source to a lower-temperature reservoir to produce work, 100% efficiency is never achieved, that is, some heat always dissipates. For example, Carnot showed that if the initial temperature is 177°C and the final is 27°C, the efficiency is 0.25. In other words, only 25% of work is performed and the remaining 75% is lost in low-temperature heat plus a minor fraction in friction. The efficiency of conversion is higher when the initial temperature (T_0) is much higher than the final temperature (T).

It is impossible to convert energy completely into work.

This is one of the ways to state the Second Law of Thermodynamics: there is a time direction in the events that occur in nature. Heat from high-temperature bodies can flow to low-temperature bodies, but the inverse does not happen. Thermal events are not reversible, while mechanical events are reversible.

More recently, other, higher-efficiency systems have been developed, such as turbines, internal combustion engines (such as Otto and Diesel engines), jet turbines, reactors, and jet rockets. Original steam engines had a maximum efficiency of 5%, but, over time and with the introduction of technical improvements, their efficiency has reached approximately 50%. Modern thermal machines such as gas turbines operate at temperatures on the order of 1,000°C and are therefore highly efficient.

What is a Sankey diagram?

A Sankey diagram is a type of flow diagram used to visualize energy, materials, cost transfers, and even movement of troops in battle. The width of the arrows is proportional to the amount of flow.

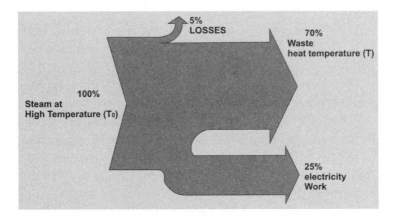

Figure 3.3 Sankey diagram for the conversion of heat into work

A graphical representation of what happens in a thermal machine can be made using a Sankey diagram (Figure 3.3).

Sankey diagrams are named after Irish Captain Matthew Henry Phineas Riall Sankey, who is considered to have been the first to use this type of diagram. He used one in 1898 in a publication on the energy efficiency of a steam engine.

Presently they are used very widely to visualize fluxes of energy from primary energy sources, through conversion to electricity and heat, and then to final energy uses. Figure 3.4 shows a simplified energy matrix for the United States.

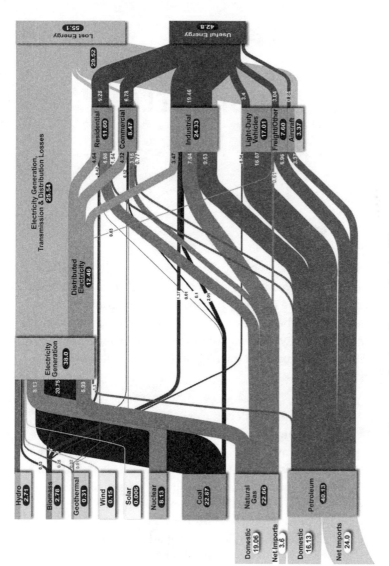

Figure 3.4 Sankey diagram for the US energy system

4

FOSSIL FUELS

What are the fossil fuels?

Fossil fuels—coal, petroleum, natural gas, and their by-products—account for approximately 85% of the world's primary energy needs today. Use of these fuels drives industrialized economies and has become an integral part of every aspect of productive activity and daily life throughout the modern world.

The resource base for gas, oil, and coal is usually split into two components:

- *Reserves*, which reflect the existing quantity of each fuel, with reasonable certainty. Reserve measurements are based on available geological and engineering data from known reservoirs and present economic and operating conditions. The lifetime of proven reserves (in years) is obtained by dividing the amount of reserves by the present yearly consumption.
- *Resources*, which reflect untapped sources of oil, gas, and coal and could extend the lifetime of reserves by a factor of 5–10. The extraction of these resources involves advanced technologies, higher costs, and possibly serious environmental problems.

Between 1869 and 2006 one-half of the proven reserves of oil were consumed, along with one-third of the natural gas reserves and approximately one-quarter of the coal reserves.

What do we know about coal?

Coal (or mineral coal) is the generic name given to a material that is produced when terrestrial plants, having been deposited underground a million years prior, undergo chemical and geological processes that give rise to turf, lignite, bituminous, and anthracite coal. The fraction of carbon found in this chain of materials increases gradually from wood (49.65%), to turf (55–44%), lignite (72.95%), bituminous coal (84.24%), and anthracite (93.50%). The heat content of these different types of fuel increases as the carbon content increases, from 4.0–4.5 kcal/kg in the turf to 7.8–9.1 kcal/kg in anthracite.

Coal usually has many impurities such as sand ash and sulfur that can reach several percent. Such impurities reduce the amount of carbon per kilogram of coal and give rise to pollutants.

Coal reserves are particularly large in North America (29.8%), Europe and Eurasia (33.0%), and the Asia Pacific (31.4%), with smaller amounts found in the other regions of the world. Total reserves in 2009 were 826 billion tons. With an annual production of 3.41 billion tons these reserves could last 251 years.

Production of electricity around the world is heavily dependent on coal; it represents 38.3% of the total electricity production (while gas represents 18.1%, nuclear 17%, hydro 16.5%, oil products 7.5%, and biomass 1.1%).

In 2008 there were 216 gigawatts (billion watts) of electricity from coal in construction in the world of which 112 gigawatts were in China.

What do we know about oil?

Petroleum (or oil) is composed of liquid hydrocarbons, and it is found in deposits that were formed, over millions of years, from oceanic animals and organic materials. Chemically, petroleum originates in the oxidation of carbohydrates (i.e., the organic matter from which it is produced). Typically the oil found in nature consists of 95–98% hydrocarbons, with sulfur impurities that can be as high as 5%. Having undergone a long evolution, oil is usually found embedded in sands or in traps in the geological formations from which it is extracted.

Oil is a complex mixture of hydrocarbons, paraffins, naphthenes, and aromatics, all of which have different boiling points. Therefore, if one warms oil, the products with lower boiling points evaporate first. This process is called distillation, and it takes place in oil refineries. Distillation of petroleum permits the separation of the different components ranging from the heaviest components (fuel oil), to diesel oil, kerosene, and gasoline. Such a process cannot alter the fraction of each one of these components but more sophisticated methods can break the heavier products, such as diesel, into lighter ones, such as gasoline. This process is called "cracking."

Petroleum has been found in many countries, but the reserves in a good number of them are either exhausted or approaching exhaustion. The largest share of remaining reserves is in the Middle East (which has 56.6% of the world's reserves); North America has 5.50% of the reserves, South and Central America 14.9%, Europe and Eurasia 10.3%, Africa 9.6%, and Asia Pacific 23.2%.

As of 2006 estimated remaining reserves of petroleum were 1.03 trillion barrels, which were being consumed at the rate of 70 million barrels per day (25.5 billion barrels per year). At this rate of consumption existing reserves should last no more than 41 years.

Such numbers refer to the reserves of the petroleum that are extracted with present technologies (or "conventional" oil). There are much larger reserves of "unconventional" oil (or very heavy oils) in sands in Alberta, Canada. Additionally, offshore oil could extend the life of the present reserves by at least another few decades.

What is abiotic oil?

There is an alternative theory about the formation of oil and gas deposits. According to it, oil is not a fossil fuel at all but was formed deep in the Earth's crust from inorganic materials. The theory argues that the formation of oil deposits requires the high pressures only found in the deep mantle and that the hydrocarbon contents in sediments do not contain sufficient organic material to supply the enormous amounts of petroleum found in very large oil fields.

The notion of abiotic oil was proposed first in the 1950s and elaborated more recently by Thomas Gold: hydrogen and carbon, under high temperature and pressures found in the mantle during the formation of the Earth formed, hydrocarbon molecules that have gradually leaked up to the Earth's surface through cracks in rocks. Furthermore, the biomarkers found in oil were produced through the metabolism of bacteria found in extreme environments similar to those in hydrothermal vents and volcanic places where it was formerly believed that life was not possible. Most geologists reject Gold's theory, which is considered controversial due to lack of clear-cut experimental evidence.

How is the price of oil evolving?

Crude oil prices behave much as any other commodity, with wide price swings in times of shortage or oversupply. The prices can also be influenced severely by the action of cartel wars or political events.

Oil was very expensive early in its use (around US$70 per barrel) but declined sharply owing to its abundance, and the price remained below US$10 per barrel for almost one century. With the October 5, 1973, start of the Yom Kippur War, fought between Israel and Syria and Egypt, OPEC—the Organization of the Petroleum Exporting Countries (whose members include Iran, Iraq, Kuwait, Saudi Arabia, Venezuela, Qatar,

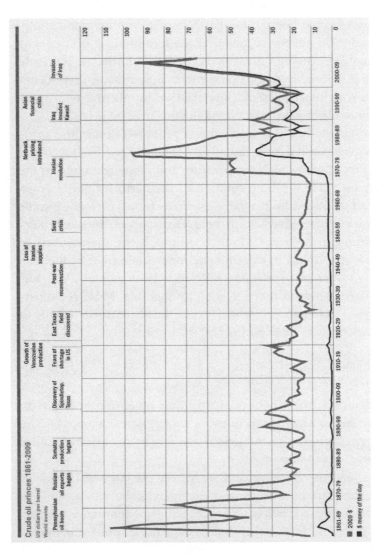

Figure 4.1 The evolution of the price of oil

Indonesia, Libya, United Arab Emirates, Algeria, and Nigeria)—imposed an embargo on oil exports to the countries supporting Israel. As a result, oil prices increased 400 percent in 6 months. This was compounded in 1979 with events in Iran and the war with Iraq, which led to another round of crude oil price increases.

Prices fell off dramatically in the 1980s, to historical levels, but has more recently increased to almost US$100 per barrel, due to upheavals in the Middle East, particularly Iraq and Libya (the main sources of the oil used in the US, Europe, and Japan). Figure 4.1 charts this evolution in the price of oil in nominal and constant 2009 dollars.

What do we know about natural gas?

Like oil, gas is trapped in porous underground rock formations, predominantly composed of sandstone. Its chief combustible component is methane (CH_4). Other energy-relevant components of natural gas include butane, ethane, and propane. Natural gas also contains small amounts of noncombustible components, including nitrogen, carbon dioxide, and hydrogen sulfide.

Commercial natural gas is generally derived from both land-based plants and marine organic matter, usually together with oil. Over geologic time, almost all natural gas migrates through the Earth's crust and eventually leaks to the atmosphere. Frequently such migration is blocked by rock formations, giving rise to reservoirs where large quantities of gas are trapped.

Gas that cannot be extracted with conventional production technology is termed "unconventional gas." The main types of unconventional gas are shale and gas hydrates.

Gas hydrate is a solid crystalline substance composed of water and natural gas (primarily methane) in which water molecules form a cage-like structure around the gas molecules. The cage structure of the hydrate molecule concentrates the component gas so that a single cubic meter of gas hydrate will yield approximately 160 cubic meters of gas. Gas hydrate forms under conditions of moderately high pressure and moderately low temperature and is widespread in marine sediments of outer continental margins and in sediments in polar regions.

Conventional natural gas reserves, as assessed by different organizations between 2007 and 2009, converge around 187.5 trillion cubic meters (Tcm) (or a thousand billion cubic meters). Production in 2009 was 3.0 Tcm. At this rate of production the reserves should last 62.5 years. The main reserves are in the Middle East (40.6%), Europe and Eurasia (40.6%), Asia Pacific (8.7%), Africa (7.9%), North America (4.9%), and South and Central America (4.3%).

Shale is a sedimentary rock consisting of clay, quartz, and other materials. It is one of the most common rock formations and can be found everywhere. However, most shale has insufficient permeability to allow significant fluid flow and, therefore, is not a suitable source of natural gas. The recent shale gas boom in North America is the result of technological advances in creating extensive artificial fractures around horizontal (rather than vertical) well bores. Within just over 10 years, the share of shale gas in US supplies rose from 0.3 Tcm in 1996 to 2 Tcm in 2008. The technology used in this case involves hydraulic fracturing of the shale reservoir in order to allow gas trapped in the rock to escape.

What is the expected life of fossil fuel reserves and resources?

Table 4.1 summarizes the situation in 2006 concerning the consumption of proven reserves of fossil fuels defined as concentration of naturally occurring solid, liquid, or gaseous material in or on the Earth's crust in such forms that economic extraction is potentially feasible. This Table also shows the present yearly consumption and the lifetime of proven reserves in years. Unconventional resources could extend the

Table 4.1 Fossil fuels reserves and consumption

		Consumption (EJ)		
	Proven reserves (EJ) end 2006	1860–2006	2006	Lifetime of proven reserves (years) at present consumption
Oil	6,888	6,380	164	41
Natural gas	7,014	3,163	109	63
Coal	19,404	6,867	130	147

Note: 1EJ = 0.15 X 10^9 barrels

lifetime of oil, gas, and coal by a factor of 5–10, but their extraction will involve advanced technologies, higher costs, and possibly serious environmental problems.

How unevenly distributed are reserves of fossil fuels around the world?

Oil and gas reserves are heavily concentrated in the Middle East: 56.6% for oil and 40.6% for gas, as shown in Table 4.2. In contrast, coal reserves are more evenly distributed: 29.8% in North America, 33% in Europe and Eurasia, and 31.4% in the Asia Pacific region. Coal is almost completely absent in the Middle East.

Table 4.2 Fossil fuel reserves in different regions of the world (in percentages)

	Oil	Gas	Coal
North America	5.5	4.9	29.8
South and Central America	14.9	4.3	1.8
Europe and Eurasia	10.3	33.7	33.0
Middle East	56.6	40.6	0.1
Africa	9.6	7.9	3.9
Asia Pacific	3.2	8.7	31.4

5

RENEWABLES

What are renewables?

Renewables, by definition, are forms of energy that are not exhaustible, as are fossil fuels. All renewables originate in the Sun and will last as long as the Sun itself. Most of them, such as wind, waves, hydroelectric, solar thermal, and biomass, originate in the radiation incident on the Earth. Tidal energy is due to the gravitational attraction between the Earth, the Sun, and the Moon, and geothermal energy originates from the center of the Earth, which has not yet cooled.

What is biomass?

Biomass is the generic name given to material generated by living organisms such as wood, charcoal, and organic residues from agriculture and animals—all of which can be used as energy sources. About 45% of biomass matter in weight is composed of carbon usually in the form of carbohydrates composed by carbon, hydrogen, and oxygen. It is abundant and, up to the middle of the 19th century, it was the dominant form of energy used by humans for home heating and cooking and heat for industrial processes. It is a renewable energy resource like all the energies originating from the Sun.

Biomass is produced continuously through photosynthesis, and one estimates that 200 billion dry tons of biomass are produced per year, of which a small fraction is used for energy purposes.

In many developing countries biomass continues to be used mainly for cooking, in very inefficient and primitive cook stoves. Still, approximately 6% of all energy consumed in the world is used for this purpose, generating some health problems related to the soot produced in inefficient burning.

The basic problem in using fuel wood to cook is its low efficiency, which is usually below 10%. This is the case of the three-stone cooking stove, widely used by low-income populations in developing countries. Although the energy produced is cheap, these stoves are very polluting and prone to accidents. Simple improvements in primitive stoves are inexpensive and may considerably increase the efficiency of the stoves. The first step to improving these stoves is a better design that would consume less fuel wood, charcoal, manure, agricultural wastes, or kerosene. Metallic stoves or stoves with thermal insulation are also up to 25% more efficient.

Through subsidies and financing, several programs in Africa, Asia, and Central America have succeeded in disseminating more efficient stoves in rural areas and in the periphery of cities, or in poorer areas.

The efficiency of cooking stoves could also be improved through a requirement that their fuel source be switched to propane (liquefied petroleum gas—LPG). Such a transition would result in a dramatic reduction in pollution: a gas stove emits 50 times fewer pollutants and is five times more efficient than a primitive stove.

The modernization of biomass usage is one of the great challenges we face, and there are already several methods for doing this, both nonbiological and biological.

Among the nonbiological processes is direct combustion of wood for the production of heat and electricity. Other processes include using charcoal for cooking and steel production, and gasification of carbon-based materials for the production of synthetic gas, methanol, or other products.

Among the main biological processes are:

- Anaerobic digestion of biodegradable materials for the production of methane, which can be done on a small scale in domestic biodigestors or on a large scale in sanitary landfills or treatment stations for urban liquid effluents;
- Fermentation of sugars (mainly from sugarcane) for the production of ethanol, used to replace gasoline in automobiles; and
- Saccharification (through enzymatic hydrolysis of cellulosic materials, such as plants) followed by fermentation of the sugar. Cellulose is made up of long strings of sugars.

Recent increases in modern biomass use have been seen in a number of European countries, particularly Austria, Denmark, Germany, Hungary, the Netherlands, Sweden, and the United Kingdom, and in some developing countries. An estimated 56 GW of biomass power capacity was in place by the end of 2009.

What are hydroelectric plants?

Large dams are usually defined as dams with a height of 15 meters or more from their foundation. If dams are between 5 and 15 meters high and have a reservoir volume of more than 3 million cubic meters, they are also classified as large dams.

Small hydro plants (mini hydro) usually generate between 1 and 30 Megawatts and have flood areas smaller than 13 square kilometers.

There are more than 45,000 large dams around the world, and they have played an important role in helping communities and economies harness water resources for food production, energy generation, flood control, and domestic use. Current estimates suggest that some 30–40% of irrigated land worldwide now relies on dams and that dams generate 16.5% of the world's electricity.

From the 1930s to the 1970s, the construction of large dams became—in the eyes of many—synonymous with development and
economic progress, and they were viewed as symbols of modernization. Thus, their construction accelerated significantly. This
trend peaked in the 1970s, when on average two or three large
dams were commissioned each day somewhere in the world.

Hydro plants usually use reservoirs to equalize the water
flows that drive the electricity-generating turbine. Water is
stored behind the dam for seasonal, annual, and, in some
cases, multiannual regulation of the river. These dams are
built, ideally, in narrow gorges, with great depth and relatively
small flood area. Examples are the Hoover Dam near the
Grand Canyon (which spurred the growth of Las Vegas) and
the dams built in the Alps. As there are few places offering
ideal dam-building conditions, dams of lesser height and
longer lengths are often built, flooding vast superficial exten-
sions. Run-of-river dams often have no storage reservoirs and
operate with encapsulated electric generators, or bulb
generators.

Large dams require significant financial investments. Estimates suggest that, worldwide, at least US$2 trillion have
been invested in the construction of large dams over the last
century. During the 1990s, an estimated US$32–46 billion was
spent annually on large dams, four-fifths of it in developing
countries. Of the US$22–31 billion invested in dams each year
in developing countries, about four-fifths were financed
directly by the public sector. The immediate benefits of large
dams, including food security considerations, local
employment and skills development, rural electrification, and
the expansion of physical and social infrastructure such as
roads, were widely believed sufficient to justify the enormous
investments made.

Presently there are approximately 1000 GW of hydroelectric power in operation and more than 150 GW under
construction. The theoretical potential for hydroelectric generation is five times larger.

What is wind energy?

Wind has been used since the most remote antiquity for navigation based on the use of sails, but it was also used to grind grains in the 7th century. In the 17th century windmills became very popular in Europe and by around 1750, there were 6,000–8,000 mills in operation in Holland, with typical powers of 7.5 kW. In the beginning of the 20th century these mills were used very extensively for water lifting and irrigation and the generation of electricity. In isolated systems, batteries are necessary to store electricity for when the wind is not blowing.

The amount of power obtained from a windmill increases rapidly with the velocity of the wind. Typical wind velocities are in the range of 3–10 m/sec, that is, 10–36 km/hour. Contrary to common belief, the average wind velocity is rather regular and fluctuations do not deviate more than 10–15% from the average wind velocity, over a year. If the wind velocity is 6 m/sec, one can generate approximately 140 W/m^2.

Modern wind machines are very large, with blades more than 80 m in length and generating approximately 5 MW. The world's installed capacity of wind machines for the production of electricity at the end of 2010 was 198 GW.

Those wanting to install wind machines sometimes meet with community resistance due to environmental problems such as noise or degradation of the scenery. To solve such problems, many wind machines are installed offshore, far from populated places.

What are photovoltaic panels?

Photovoltaic (PV) cells, discovered in 1954 by Bell Laboratories researchers, convert solar energy directly into electricity. The incident solar radiation (or photons) displaces free electrons from the semiconductor material; when the electrons leave their positions, the imbalance of the electric charges at the front and at the back of the cells generates a difference in potential, in turn generating an electric current. This is what happens in conventional lead-acid batteries. One can visualize the process by thinking of a garage that has two levels and is so completely full of cars that they cannot move. If one removes one of the cars to an upper level, the remaining cars in the lower level can move. The movement of the cars is the analogy to an electric current. A photovoltaic module is composed of cell panels, each having a width of 1–10 cm and producing 1–2 W. The current generated is continuous, which is ideal for small appliances, but can be converted into alternating current for larger equipment.

Historically, photovoltaic power was applied in niches and special applications, such as isolated communities, electronic equipment (calculators, watches, and communication technology), satellites, remote sensing, and sign lighting along roads. The problem with niche applications is that it is done on a small scale and at a high cost. Large-scale production is required for cost reduction. In places with high insolation, 5,000 kWh of power a day could be produced over a hectare of land covered with photocells with 10% efficiency. Some commercial cells have an efficiency of 15%. The installation of PV panels is rapidly growing and the power generation potential of photovoltaic panels is promising. One idea is that power from buildings with solar roofs could be "fed-in" to the electricity grid. PVs may be one of the main technologies for future decentralized energy systems.

By the end of 2010 there were 40 GW of installed PV systems. Germany is the present market leader, leading Japan and the US. Previously, Japan was the group leader in PV modules technology, concentrating on the consumer market niche of electronic products (such as calculators and watches). The North American industry traditionally concentrates on large-scale applications. Other important suppliers are China, Spain, and Italy. The limiting factors of photovoltaic power are its cost, the limited power produced per unit, and the lack of available silicon in the market. Photovoltaic panel manufacturing requires large amounts of polycrystalline silicon and there is now a supply bottleneck, which constrains the technology expansion. Each Wp (watt peak) consumes 14 g of silicon. Still, the present installed cost for photovoltaic systems connected to the grid is lower than US$2,000/kW.

In remote rural areas, which cannot be connected to the grid, PV modules are used together with batteries, charge controllers, and inverters. Despite being small, the power produced is enough to refrigerate medicines; preserve food and fishing products; light houses, schools, and medical centers; extract and pump water from wells; and support communication and entertainment. The disposal of batteries and panels is a problem, as they contain lead and other dangerous heavy metals such as cadmium. Another severe problem is lack of maintenance; this frequently occurs in demonstration projects focused only on installation of a system, with no adequate technical assistance or spare parts.

What is solar thermal energy?

Solar equipment for heating water is usually passive. In this process, solar light is absorbed in a panel at the top of a building reservoir, through which water circulates. The warmed water is then stored and distributed. The collectors are panels covered with glass, under which water circulates in metallic tubes. Frequently there is an auxiliary electric or gas system to heat the water in the reservoir when it falls below 50°C (122°F), such as during periods when the Sun is not shining or covered by clouds or in the winter.

Solar energy has been used for many years to heat water. Countries such as Israel and cities such as Barcelona in Spain have enacted mandatory laws and incentive programs for the installation of panels, which efficiently replaces the use of fossil fuels and fuel wood for heating. In hot climates, solar heating may satisfy approximately 75% of the demand for water heating. In the cold climate of Europe, this proportion falls to about 20%, or even less. China managed to popularize a low-cost solar water heating system, with prices cheaper than in the Western countries: US$120–US$150/m² versus US$700–US$800/m² in Europe. In China, at least 30 million users had thermal heaters in 2006.

What is solar thermoelectricity?

In this technology sunlight is focused on a collector to heat a fluid to a few hundred degrees Celsius, producing steam for electricity generation. The most popular technology to do this uses parabolic mirrors, which are large mirrors shaped in such a way that they concentrate the solar rays incident on them on a pipe placed at the center of the curved surfaces, where a circulating fluid is heated. The existing projects are still marginally competitive, and research and development are still needed in this area. Large-scale power plants using parabolic mirrors operate in California (at a power of 350 MW). Spain intends to start operating two units soon, totaling 100 MW, and has more than 1,000 MW in final design phase.

What is wave energy?

The oscillation of the surface of the sea, caused by winds, can be used to drive mechanical devices that generate electricity. The energy potential that can be obtained is very large (2.5 million MW), but the technology needed to do this is in its infancy. The main reason is the low density of energy: if the typical length of ocean waves is 60 m and their maximum height is 3 m, the maximum power one can obtain is 36 W/m along the coastline. To generate 1,000 kW, one would need devices with a length of 30 km. It is presently prohibitively expensive to capture this energy.

What is tidal energy?

The gravitational pull of the Earth–Moon system produces tides, or the rise and fall of the ocean level, twice every 24 h. Usually the rise is small (approximately 1 m), but, occasionally, depending of the geography of the coastal area, there can be larger rises in bays and estuaries.

The most spectacular of such phenomena takes place in the Fundy Bay in Nova Scotia, Canada. At the entrance of the bay the tide rise is 5 m, but at the end of the bay it reaches 13 m.

This movement of the great masses of ocean water can be used to generate hydroelectricity. The most important commercial use of tidal energy, presently, takes place in La Rance, France, where the bay has an area of 22 km^2 and produces approximately 250 MW of hydroelectricity.

The world's potential for the production of electricity from tides is estimated to be 3 million MW.

What is geothermal energy?

Geothermal energy is the energy that originates from the hot nucleus of the Earth. As is well known if one drills a well, the temperature increases approximately 2 °C per every 100 m in depth. Therefore, at a depth of 10 km the temperature is 200 °C and can be used to produce steam and thus generate electricity. There are, however, "hot spots" or geysers near volcanic regions where hot water or water vapor is produced naturally on the surface of the Earth, at high pressure and temperature, making it easier to generate electricity. The first geothermal energy plant was installed in Larderello, Italy, in 1904, and started to produce 250 MW in 1912.

The world's installed capacity for geothermal energy at the end of 2009 was 86 GW electric and 49 GWh thermal. Electricity generated amounted to 47.5 TWh.

What is the potential of renewable energies?

The theoretical potential of renewables is enormous; this potential is approximately 5 million EJ/year, or almost 10,000 times more than present consumption of 500 EJ/year. There are, however, problems encountered in converting this potential to usable form, so the technical potential is much smaller than the theoretical potential but still considerable. In contrast, the amount of renewables being used today is small, as indicated in Table 5.1. It is approximately 62 EJ/year, mostly in the form of biomass, so there are enormous opportunities for increasing the use of renewable forms of energy.

How much land is needed to produce energy from renewables?

Concerns have been raised over the amount of area needed to produce large amounts of renewable energy as compared to the amount needed to produce fossil fuels, which have a very large energy density. One can produce approximately 3 kWh per kilogram of fossil fuels, an amount which would fit in a small cubic box of less than 10 cm on each side. To generate the same amount of electricity from photovoltaics, one would

Table 5.1 Renewable energy production, technical and theoretical potentials

	Technical potential (EJ/year)	Theoretical potential (EJ/year)	Production (EJ/year)
Solar	62,000–280,000	3,900,000	0.49
Wind	1,250–2,250	110,000	0.98
Hydro	53–57	160	11.23
Biomass	160–270	1,330	50.3
Geothermal	810–1,545	1,500	0.49
Ocean	3,200–10,500	1,000,000	0.01

need typically 50 m² of surface over the course of a day. The area needs for renewables is therefore very large and could lead to space limitations.

The production of biomass energy also requires a large amount of space since photosynthesis is an inherently inefficient energy-conversion process. Even with an intensively cultivated plantation of fast-growing trees, a wood-burning electricity generation plant would not have power densities higher than 0.6 W/m². Space demand for such facilities, then, would be two to three orders of magnitude (100 to 1,000 times) greater than for coal- or gas-fired electricity generation.

Photovoltaic plants can generate electricity with much higher power densities than wood-burning stations. Converting solar radiation to new biomass, overall, has an efficiency no better than 1%, while even relatively inefficient PV cells have efficiencies around 5%, and today's best commercial facilities go above 10%. Taking only the PV cell area into consideration, this translates to power densities of mostly between 10 and 20 W/m². But when all ancillary space requirements are included, the typical density range declines to 4–9 W/m², an order of magnitude higher than for wood-powered generation but one to three orders of magnitude lower (that is demanding 10 to 1,000 times more space) than the common modes of fossil fuel electricity production.

Power densities for central solar power are slightly higher, with rates as high as 45–55 W/m², when only the area of solar collectors is considered, but with overall power densities (including spacing, access roads, and tower facilities) on the order of 10 W/m². Finally, wind-driven electricity generation has power densities similar to, or slightly higher than, wood-burning stations, with most new installations using powerful (1–6 MW) turbines fitting into a range between 0.5 and 1.5 W/m².

For power plants alone such densities are commonly in excess of 2 kW/m² and can be as high as 5 kW/m². When all other requirements (coal mining, storage, environmental controls, settling ponds) are included, the densities inevitably decline and range over an order of magnitude from as low as 100 W/m² to as much as 1,000 W/m² (1 kW/m²).

In contrast, compact gas turbine plants, which can be connected to existing gas supplies, can generate electricity with power density as high as 15 kW/m². Larger stations (>100 MW) using the most efficient combined-cycle arrangements (with a gas turbine's exhaust used to generate steam for an attached steam turbine) will operate with lower power densities. If new natural gas extraction capacities have to be developed for their operation, then the overall power density of gas and electricity production would decline to a range similar to that of coal-fired thermal generation or slightly higher, in most cases to a range of 200–2,000 W/m² (Table 5.2).

Most of the area occupied by large wind farms could be used for crops or grazing but other land uses would be excluded, and large areas dotted with wind turbines would require construction and maintenance of access roads as well as the creation of buffer zones not suitable for permanent human habitation. And in all cases of renewable energy conversion, much more land would be needed for more extensive transmission rights-of-way in order to export electricity

Table 5.2 Typical power density of energy sources

Power source	Power density (W/m²)	
	Low	High
Natural gas	200	2,000
Coal	100	1,000
Solar (PV)	4	9
Solar (CSP)	4	10
Wind	0.5	1.5
Biomass	0.5	0.6

from sunny and windy regions, or from areas suited for mass-scale biomass production, to major urban and industrial areas.

What are the prospects for increased use of renewables?

Presently new renewables (modern biomass energy, geothermal heat and electricity, small hydropower, low-temperature solar heat, and wind electricity) contribute approximately 2% to the world's total primary energy supply.

However, electricity production from solar photovoltaic systems as well as grid-connected wind turbines has been growing at an impressive rate. Between 1998 and 2008 wind electricity grew at an average rate of approximately 30%, while grid connected photovoltaic energy grew by almost 40%, bioethanol by 13%, and geothermal heat production by 20%. Even so, it will likely be decades before new renewables add up to a major fraction of total global energy use because they currently represent only a small percentage of total energy use. Nevertheless, a few countries have adopted ambitious targets; Germany, for example, has a target of 50% renewables by 2050. Impressive growth rates have been achieved in recent years for geothermal (in Iceland) and solar thermal heat production (in China).

Substantial cost reductions in the past few decades have made a number of renewable energy technologies competitive with fossil fuel technologies in certain applications. Modern, distributed forms of biomass, in particular, have the potential to provide rural areas with clean forms of energy based on the use of biomass resources that have traditionally been used in inefficient, polluting ways. Biomass can be economically produced with minimal or even positive environmental impacts through perennial crops. Its production and use is currently helping to create international bioenergy markets, stimulated by policies to reduce carbon dioxide emissions. Wind power in coastal and other windy regions is promising in the short term as well. Other potentially attractive options include geothermal heat and electricity production, small hydropower, low-temperature solar heat production, and solar electricity production in remote applications.

Substantial cost reductions can be achieved for most renewable energy technologies. Making these renewable energy sources competitive will require further technological development and market deployment and an increase in production capacities to mass-production levels.

A negative aspect of some renewables is that, unlike hydropower and geothermal power sources, wind and solar thermal or electric sources are intermittent and not fully predictable. Nevertheless, they can be important in rural areas where grid extension is expensive. They can also contribute to grid-connected electricity supplies in appropriate configurations; intermittent renewables can reliably provide 10–30% of total electricity supplies in an area covered by a sufficiently strong transmission grid if operated in conjunction with hydropower or fuel-based power generation. Emerging storage possibilities (like compressed-air energy storage) and new strategies for operating grids offer promise that the role of intermittent technologies can be extended much further. Alternatively, hydrogen may become the medium for storing intermittently available energy production.

Because they are small in scale and modular, many renewable technologies are good options for continued cost cutting. Cost reductions for manufactured goods are typically rapid at first and then taper off as the industry matures.

6

NUCLEAR POWER

What is nuclear power?

Nuclear power is not based on mechanical energy (as is hydropower) or chemical energy (as is the burning of fossil fuels). Nuclear energy is created by the splitting of the nuclei of uranium atoms. This splitting releases a considerable amount of kinetic energy in radioactive fragments such as strontium (Sr) and xenon (Xe). This process is called "nuclear fission" and can be induced by bombarding uranium atoms with suitable projectiles such as neutrons. Nuclear fission is followed by neutron or proton emission and by radiation, such as X-rays. The final fragments, the nuclear waste, are highly radioactive, and thus are one of the serious problems resulting from the use of this type of energy.

In the fission of a uranium atom by a neutron, 2.5 other neutrons are produced, on the average all of which can, in turn, produce other fissions, creating a chain reaction that leads to the fission of a huge amount of other atoms. If this process happens quickly, it produces a nuclear explosion, which is basically a large number of uranium atoms undergoing fission in a short period. If the process is slowed down, then large quantities of heat are produced as the kinetic energy of the fragments dissipates. In a nuclear reactor this heat is removed and used to boil water and the vapor generated is used to produce electricity, as it is done in thermal power generation stations that burn fuel wood, coal, or gas.

Table 6.1 Comparison of the power generated from
different energy sources

Fuel	Power (kWh) generated by 1 Kg of fuel	Amount required (tons a year) for a 1,000 MWe thermoelectricity plant
Fuel wood	1	3,400,000
Coal	3	2,700,000
Fuel oil	4	2,000,000
Uranium	50,000	30

The energy released by nuclear fission is large compared to the energy produced in the burning of such fuels, which is why it is possible to generate large quantities of electricity with small amounts of uranium. For example, 1 kg of uranium "burned" in a nuclear reactor can produce 50,000 kWh, while 1 kg of coal can produce only 1 kWh (Table 6.1).

Of the uranium found in nature only 0.7% can be used in a nuclear reactor. Put another way, only 7 out of every 1,000 atoms of uranium are "useful" for the production of energy. For this reason the preparation of nuclear fuel requires a complex "fuel cycle," beginning with the extraction and purification of uranium salts, and then to their conversion to a gas and the "enrichment" of the uranium into the fissionable isotope ^{235}U. Once enriched uranium rods are prepared, they constitute the core of the nuclear reactors for electricity production.

The coolant in a reactor takes away the heat generated in the fission process, limiting the temperature rise in the rectors. It also transfers the heat to the power unit, where the electricity is generated.

There are basically two types of nuclear reactors: boiling water reactors (BWR), which produce vapor inside the reactor, and pressurized water reactors (PWR), which pressurize hot water (rather than boiling it) while removing the heat.

In 2010, there were 442 reactors worldwide, producing 14% of the world's electricity. Out of these, 104 are in the United States, 50 in France, 54 in Japan, 32 in the Russian Federation, 21 in South Korea, and 17 in Germany. In the United States they represented 19% of the total generated electricity and in France approximately 80%. The remaining reactors are installed in developing countries, mainly in China and India. The total installed capacity in the world is approximately the same as for hydroelectric-generating units.

The percentage of the world's electricity produced by nuclear energy has been declining in recent years. New grid connections peaked at 30 GW/yr in the mid-1980s, and the last decade has witnessed a decline to 5 GW/yr or less. Efforts are being made to extend the life of existing plants and to stimulate the building of new ones so as to promote "a nuclear renaissance" and thereby sustain the share of nuclear energy in a growing global electric power sector. This is what the Nuclear Energy Agency of the Organization for Economic Co-operation and Development (OECD) and the International Atomic Energy Agency feel is achievable prior to 2050.

Why has the growth of nuclear energy declined since 1985?

The construction of most of the existing reactors began before 1975 and was completed by 1985. After the incidents at Three Mile Island, in the United States in 1978, and Chernobyl, currently in Ukrainian territory, in 1986, construction of new reactors declined dramatically.

The reasons for this decline are complex and involve economic, environmental, and political concerns. For one thing, economies of scale have driven up the size of the present generation of nuclear reactors, most of which are in the gigawatt range, requiring several billions of dollars in investments. Relatedly, the increases in safety requirements and decommissioning costs also affect the economic feasibility of nuclear power. As opposed to other technologies and against optimistic predictions, nuclear power has not been shown to follow a "learning curve" process whereby costs decrease with economies of scale. Furthermore, there are political concerns, mostly related to the danger of nuclear proliferation, since nuclear technology is basically a dual technology allowing diversion of enriched uranium or plutonium for the manufacture of nuclear weapons. There are also problems related to nuclear waste disposal.

What are the problems of nuclear waste disposal?

Elements removed from a reactor after its use correspond to less than 1% of the waste volume, but they contain 95% of the total radioactivity. Radioactive atoms are unstable and emit particles or radiation ("decay") until they are transformed into stable atoms. This is a statistical process and it is characterized by a half-life, which is the time needed for half of the radioactive atoms to "decay." During this process, the nuclear waste activity is reduced by 90% in the first year, but 100,000 years are necessary for it to revert to uranium ore levels. Uranium-235 fission generates radioactive isotopes of xenon and strontium (among others), which undergo radioactive decays until stable components are formed. Some of these intermediary products—particularly strontium-90 and cesium-137, with half-lives of about 30 years—are very carcinogenic and persistent in the environment, so much so that they can settle in people's bones.

Nuclear waste has to be stored for many decades, and maybe centuries, in deep underground reservoirs, in stable geological formations on solid ground, or on the sea bed and contained in cement, bitumen, and resins for vitrification. There is still no final storage capacity for these materials. The United States had plans to build a permanent large nuclear waste depository, with a 70,000 ton capacity, in Yucca Mountain by 2019. The estimated cost to build the storage site was between US$10 billion and US$20 billion. However, owing to opposition by environmental groups, the US administration stopped the project in 2010. Finland is building a smaller depository to store the nuclear waste from its reactors. France has provisory nuclear waste disposal sites. In the United States the waste produced by the more than 100 reactors in operation is presently being stored in concrete blocks or water-filled pools at the reactor sites.

What is the nuclear "renaissance"?

The greenhouse gas emissions from nuclear energy production—over a life cycle—are very low, because nuclear plants do not burn fossil fuels. The main source of such emissions comes from the energy utilized in the construction of the nuclear reactor site and the preparation of the nuclear fuel. Reactor operations also have negligible emissions of sulfur dioxide (SO_2) and nitrous oxides (NO_x), the pollutants emitted by burning fossil fuels. Therefore, from the environmental viewpoint nuclear reactors as a source of electricity production are attractive, and the recent increased concerns with global warming led to strong efforts to revitalize the nuclear industry.

Uranium reserves are abundant and can cost less than US$40/kgU to extract. Reserves in 2009 at that cost amounted to 570 thousand tons and production amounted to 44 thousand tons, so, in principle, they should last for only 13 years. At higher costs of production (lower than US$80/kgU) reserves jump to 2.5 million tons.

Reserves, resources, and occurrences of uranium are based on a once-through fuel cycle operation. Closed fuel cycles and breeding technology would increase the uranium resource dimension 50–60 fold. Thorium-based fuel cycles would enlarge the fissile resource base further.

If the other problems related to the use of nuclear energy, such as nuclear waste disposal and nuclear proliferation, are resolved, nuclear energy could contribute more to the energy supply in the 21st century.

Several countries, particularly the United States, have attempted to stimulate a "nuclear renaissance" in the last few years. Until the end of 2010 there were signs of such a "renaissance," with the start of construction of a few new reactors, mainly in China, Russia, and Eastern Europe. In addition to that, some 50 developing countries indicated their interest in installing nuclear reactors, although many of them do not have electricity grids large enough to accommodate large nuclear units, which are very expensive.

These plans have been put in question by the nuclear accident in Fukushima, Japan, where six reactors were severely hit by an earthquake followed by a tsunami. The consequences were very serious due to the partial melting of some of the fuel rods at the core of the reactor and a release of radioactive Cesium 137 greater than 15% of the emissions in the Chernobyl disaster and more than 100 times the amount released by the Hiroshima atomic bomb. This release of radioactivity forced the evacuation of hundreds of thousands of people living in a radius of 20 kilometers of the Fukushima plant. The accident was classified as a level 7 on the scale of gravity of nuclear accidents, which is at the same levels as the one in Chernobyl.

Worldwide the Fukushima accident led to a tightening of security measures to avoid the repetition of such disasters and a general reappraisal of the future role of nuclear energy in the world energy matrix.

Several OECD countries (Germany, Belgium, Italy, and Switzerland) decided to phase out existing reactors at the end of their useful life and cancelled plans for new ones. Japan cancelled plans for new reactors. The International Energy Agency reduced by 50% its projection for the number of new reactors (approximately 200) planned to be installed by 2035. China has halted expansion plans pending a review of safety procedures.

What is nuclear fusion?

Nuclear fusion is a nuclear reaction in which two (or more) light atomic nuclei fuse to form a heavier one. It is the opposite of nuclear fission, in which a heavy nucleus such as uranium splits into two lighter fragments releasing a considerable amount of energy (and radioactive products).

A fusion reaction occurs only when the interacting nuclei come very close together, which is difficult because they are both positively charged and there is a strong repulsion among them. Therefore, fusion can only occur at very high temperatures where the nuclei have high velocities. There were claims that it was possible to achieve "cold fusion" at room temperature, but they were not confirmed independently.

Fusion occurs naturally in stars, including the Sun. This is the origin of the solar radiation that reaches the Earth. Scientists are attempting controlled nuclear fusion in laboratories in order to produce electricity, but there are numerous technological problems with the process that have yet to be solved. The great advantage of nuclear fusion over nuclear fission for the production of energy is that in the fusion reaction very little nuclear waste is produced.

PART III

THE PROBLEMS OF THE PRESENT
ENERGY SYSTEM

7

EXHAUSTION OF FOSSIL FUELS AND ENERGY SECURITY

Are fossil fuels being exhausted?

Although fossil fuel reserves are very large, they are, by nature, exhaustible. As we have discussed previously, the expected life of presently identified reserves is 41 years for oil, 63 years for natural gas, and 147 years for coal. Among them, oil is clearly the more convenient to use because it can easily be stocked and transported. Present transportation systems are almost entirely dependent on the use of petroleum derivatives.

What experience shows is that production is peaking in a number of countries, raising questions about the "end of oil." Non-OPEC, non-FSU (former Soviet Union countries) oil production was first explored at the beginning of the last century and peaked around 2000. It is currently declining, according to many sources.

Estimates state that approximately one-half of the existing oil reserves, 0.92 trillion barrels, were used up between 1860 and 2006. The remaining 1.03 trillion barrels remain to be explored.

Nevertheless, the issue of how large oil reserves are is a very controversial one because oil exploration is intimately linked with the technologies involved as well as costs.

The "end of oil" means that nonconventional reserves will have to be tapped and explored at greater cost. Enhanced-oil-recovery technologies will be needed for deepwater exploration to recover oil reserves in the Artic, heavy oil bitumen, and oil shales.

The use of such resources might result in additional environmental problems such as large oil spills in offshore exploration, very well illustrated by the recent Gulf of Mexico BP disaster. The extraction of shale oil in Canada is another example of fossil fuel exploration that led to new environmental problems.

What is the "peak oil debate"?

There is a deep divide between geologists and economists over trying to answer the question of how much oil, gas, coal, or uranium the Earth's crust holds.

An increasing number of resource geologists expect the production of oil resources to end in the not so distant future, that is, over the next 10–20 years. The geologists base their projections on the fact that oil must first be found before it can be produced. The heydays of large oil discoveries ("super giants") ended in the mid-1960s, followed by a substantial decline in the discovery of new reserves globally. Between 1980 and 2007 only 82% of global oil production was replenished by new oil reserve additions.

Continuously producing more oil without locating new reserves will eventually result in peak oil production at the approximate time when half of the oil reserves have been produced. After the peak is reached, the global availability of oil will decline year after year at a rate that depends on the rate of production. Therefore, the assumed ultimate global oil reserve endowment is a critical parameter in determining both the level of peak production and the point in time when the peak will occur. Estimated recoverable oil has routinely been calculated since the mid 20th century from the world's original endowment of conventional oil. The approximately 100 different estimates cover a wide range, especially those made during the 1970s. The majority, however, lie in the 12.6–16.7 zetajoule (ZJ) bracket. By the end of 2008 cumulative oil production amounted to some 6.5 ZJ (156 Gtoe). Going by the lower estimates, we have almost reached the half-way production mark (the peak), and production is bound to decline from here on out. Using the higher estimates would only shift the peak by a decade or so.

The term "recoverable" is not a definite measurement for "oil-in-place" but only the portion that is recoverable because of geological complexities and economic limitations. One technology for mining more oil is enhanced recovery (EOR), which is applied to extract residual amounts of oil that otherwise would not reach the surface. Another one is offshore extraction at increasingly deeper depths, where the oil is sometimes covered by very tricky salt deposits.

Economists believe that technological innovation will continue to allow exploration of additional reserves not currently identified, or not economically extractable with existing technology. Higher prices not only push the frontier of marketable resources (smaller field, higher recovery rates, more challenging environments, etc.) but stimulate upstream technology and R&D in exploration and production.

Economists claim that the immensity and importance of the world's unconventional sources of oil are rarely acknowledged, and that the quantities reported are based on static technology. When (conventional and unconventional) oil production hits a maximum sustainable level, production is likely to be characterized by an "undulating plateau," rather than by a peak, followed by a sharp drop-off in output. The trajectory of future oil production is shown in Figure 7.1.

Geologists counter that even if the resource base of nonconventional oil will be tapped, production would be constrained by high specific investment and production costs, as well as environmental regulation. Such constraints are likely to cap production significantly. In sum, global oil supply is

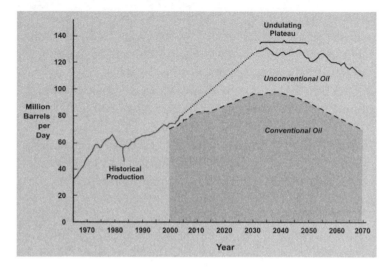

Figure 7.1 The future of oil production

going to peak and start its inevitable decline at higher and higher oil prices.

Differences in recoverable estimates and the role of technology and price explain the variations in time and volume. Both geologists and economists see a role for unconventional oil in future oil supply. However, they disagree about the rate at which it can be developed and over the degree of economic and environmental costs.

There are studies of coal and gas similar to the ones made for oil, but the reserves for such sources of energy are very large—and for the case of natural gas is even growing—so such concerns are less urgent.

What is energy security?

Uninterrupted provision of vital energy services—a proxy for "energy security"—is a high priority of every nation. For most industrialized countries energy security is related to import dependency and aging infrastructure, while many emerging economies have additional vulnerabilities such as insufficient technical capacity and rapid demand for growth. In many low-income countries, supply and demand vulnerabilities overlap, making them especially insecure.

This situation is particularly serious with regard to oil and its derivatives, which provide at least 90% of the transport energy needs in almost all countries that lack available substitutes. Furthermore, the global demand for transport fuels is steadily rising, especially in Asian emerging economies. Disruptions of oil supplies may thus result in catastrophic effects on food production, medical care, security, and other vital functions of modern states.

The remaining oil resources are increasingly geographically concentrated in just a few countries and regions, which means that most countries must import an ever higher share or even all of their oil needs. Over 3 billion people live in 83 countries that import more than 75% of the oil products they consume. An additional 1.7 billion people live in countries with limited domestic oil resources and are likely to experience similarly high levels of import dependency in the next decade or two. The increasing concentration of conventional oil production and the rapidly shifting global demand patterns make some analysts and politicians fear a "scramble for energy" or even "resource wars."

Import dependency is also common in countries that rely on natural gas to provide heat and generate electricity. Almost 650 million people live in 32 Eurasian countries that import over 75% of their gas needs. In addition, 12 countries with some 780 million people rely on limited domestic gas reserves and are thus likely to experience significant import dependency in the future. Short-term supply disruptions and rapid price increases are often the most serious energy security issues, especially in those countries that rely on a single supplier and a limited number of pipelines to import natural gas.

Costs of energy (primarily oil) imports exceed 20% of export earnings in 35 countries, with 2.5 billion people, and they exceed 10% of GDP in an additional 15 countries with 200 million people.

These vulnerabilities in electricity supply are often made worse by demand-side pressures. The majority of the world population—some 4.2 billion people—live in 53 countries. These countries will need to massively expand the capacity of their electricity systems in the near future because they either have less than 60% access to electricity or average demand growth of over 6% during the last decade. Both fuels and infrastructure for such an expansion will need to be provided without further compromising sovereignty or resilience of national electricity systems.

What are the problems of access to energy services in the developing countries?

Poverty—linked to low income—is often perceived as the most critical social challenge that needs to be addressed in considering problems of access to energy. The latest comprehensive estimates indicate that about 2.6 billion people live on less than US$2 a day. Out of this population, about 1.4 billion live in extreme poverty, accounting for the bulk of the 1.5 billion people with no access to electricity.

Over 2.5 billion people rely on traditional biomass, such as fuel wood, charcoal, agricultural waste, and animal dung, to meet their energy needs for cooking. This number is projected to rise from 2.7 billion today to 2.8 billion in 2030.

The vast majority of the population living in extreme poverty have limited access to modern energy and cleaner energy options such as electricity or modern cooking fuels such as liquid petroleum gas (LPG). Enhanced access to modern and cleaner energy options can become an effective tool for combating extreme hunger by increasing food productivity and reducing post-harvest losses. In both cases, the energy technologies required to meet the objectives can often be produced locally. An example is irrigation, which requires substantial electricity inputs that can be obtained from wind pumps or photovoltaic panels.

Electricity in rural health centers enables provision of medical services at night as well as assisting in retaining qualified staff and allowing the use of more advanced medical equipment (for example, sterilization and refrigeration of medicines). In addition, energy is needed to develop, manufacture, and distribute drugs, medicine, and vaccinations as well as enable access to health education media through information and communications technologies (ICT).

To meet the more ambitious target of achieving universal access to modern energy services by 2030, additional investment of $756 billion, or $36 billion per year, is required according to recent estimates. This is less than 3% of the global energy investment projected for 2030. The resulting increase in primary energy demand and CO_2 emissions would be modest.

While the scale of the challenge is tremendous, access to energy, electricity, and modern fuels and/or stoves for all is achievable by 2030. Such an achievement will require global investments of about US$16–65 billion annually, a small fraction of the total costs of energy infrastructure.

Access to modern cooking fuels may contribute to little or no rise in greenhouse gas emissions. Immediate benefits include improved health on the order of 800,000–1.8 million avoided deaths a year, a decrease in the amount of people's time spent on cooking, and the socioeconomic benefits from improved energy access. Such benefits will extend well beyond the current generation.

8

ENVIRONMENTAL PROBLEMS

Why are environmental problems so important today?

In a short period (about 150 years after the Industrial Revolution), the environmental impacts, in terms of magnitude, of human activities became comparable to the ones caused by natural effects. Humans have become a force of geological proportions. For example, natural forces (such as wind, erosion, rain, volcanic eruptions) move about 50 million tons of material a year. The present population of the Earth uses an average of 8 tons of mineral resources per capita per year, moving about 48 billion tons. A century ago, the world population was 1.5 billion and the amount of resources used was smaller than 2 tons per capita: the total impact was 16 times smaller. As a result of this increased impact, new problems or areas of interest in the environmental field have turned into an object of study and concern.

The environmental problems are usually grouped into three categories:

- Local
- Regional, and
- Global.

Local pollution deals with clean air, fresh supplies of clean water, the removal and disposal of solid wastes and liquid effluents, street cleaning, and so on. Such activities have characterized "good" small and medium sized cities since Roman times. Yet in many developing countries, a large fraction of the population lives among the rubble and residues it produces, owing to the lack of resources to remove waste and to build sewers and engineer works for the supply of water. This is quite evident in the slums of the big cities that, generally speaking, surround "islands of prosperity," where the well-to-do succeed in obtaining a quality of life that is comparable to that of Europe or the United States. Local pollution goes hand in hand with poverty and is usually dealt with by local governments.

Regional pollution is caused mainly by automobiles, energy production, and heavy industry, which are inherent to more prosperous societies. Large cities and adjoining areas, such as Los Angeles, Mexico City, and São Paulo, have long been "suffocating" under the pollution caused by the emissions and smog resulting from the burning of fossil fuels. Sometimes the amount of pollution produced is large enough to cause regional and even transborder problems, such as the "acid rain" that originated in the United States but was responsible for the destruction of life in Canadian lakes. The same has happened to lakes in Scandinavia, owing to industrial activities on the other side of the Baltic Sea. Regional pollution has to be dealt with at the state or national level and eventually among a number of countries.

Global pollution is the third category and its most obvious consequences to date are the destruction of the stratospheric ozone layer (or "shield") by CFCs (chlorofluorocarbons) and the "greenhouse effect." These problems result from changes in the composition of the atmosphere and have little to do with national borders. The causes of such global problems are gases, which can originate from anywhere in the world. For example, the well-being of people living in Switzerland might ultimately be affected by what takes place in India or China (and vice versa). Global pollution can only be tackled at the international level.

The classification of environmental problems as local, regional, and global is somewhat arbitrary because some problems that start as local ones can easily become of regional and even global significance. Oil spills, which are commonplace but frequently acquire enormous visibility, constitute one example.

Which are the local environmental problems?

Local environmental problems are of three types:

Urban air pollution results mainly from the pollutants emitted by automobiles and trucks using gasoline and diesel oil. Examples of pollutants include emissions of sulfur dioxide (SO_2), carbon monoxide (CO), nitrogen oxides (NO_x), and particulate matter (PM) resulting from the burning of fossil fuels, especially oil and coal, as well as from electricity generation and industry.

Indoor air pollution and emissions of PM and CO result from the use of solid fuels (biomass and coal) for heating and cooking and toxic emissions from industrial and manufacturing processes.

Pollution of superficial water bodies (rivers, lakes, estuaries) and groundwater and contamination of soils are caused by leakages of oil by-products, use of fertilizers and pesticides in agriculture, leakages from filling stations, and other industrial wastes. Abandoned industrial and mining areas that lack appropriate decommissioning operations (cleanup, isolation and storage, recovery) can also contribute significantly.

What is urban air pollution?

Urban air pollution is probably the most visible undesirable product of civilization. It was an issue even in the 16th century, when British Parliament sessions in London had to be postponed due to the severe pollution "episodes" resulting from the use of fuel wood and coal for residential heating. The soot and particulates emitted act as cluster for water vapor in the atmosphere, creating thick fog. One of the most serious incidences occurred in 1952, when very heavy fog in London resulted in 4,000 deaths and more than 20,000 cases of illness. The pollution of the Thames River was a significant contributor. Such disasters led to passage of the UK Clean Air Act of 1956, establishing limits on the emission of pollutants and acceptable levels of air quality. Other legislation followed in the United Kingdom, North America, many other western European countries, and Japan. As a result, monitoring, regulatory, and assessment agencies on environmental quality were set up, with highly beneficial consequences.

The five main urban air pollutants are:

- Sulfur oxides (SO_x, mainly SO_2);
- Nitrogen oxides (NO_x and mainly nitric oxide (NO) and nitrogen dioxide (NO_2));
- Carbon monoxide (CO);
- Particulate matter—PM (including heavy metals such as lead); and
- Ozone (O_3).

Energy systems are the main source of sulfur dioxide emissions (constituting 90% of total emissions). Emissions of SO_2, which combine with water vapor in the atmosphere to produce sulfuric acid rain, have decreased in developed regions over the past two decades, while those in developing regions have increased.

In industrialized regions, industry and transportation are the main sources of CO_2 emissions. Combustion of fossil fuels and the burning of wood as fuel contribute to about one-third of total human made emissions. In developing regions inefficient combustion in primitive stoves, furnaces, and boilers is a main source.

What is indoor air pollution?

There are three types of problems related to indoor air pollution:

- Traditional—due to cooking, generally indoors, which produces smoke, particulates, carbon monoxide, and other gases mainly affecting the rural poor. More than 1 billion people in developing countries are victims of this type of pollution.
- Occupational—leading to illnesses such as silicosis and mercury poisoning, particularly victimizing miners and industrial workers.
- Modern—affecting people living in modern, airtight buildings due to radon and asbestos from building materials and formaldehyde emitted from insulating foam (the so-called sick building syndrome).

We shall restrict our discussion to the "traditional" type of pollution, which is closely linked to the fuel wood crisis.

In 1989, the total production of wood, that is, wood felled and harvested from trees regardless of its use, was about 3,500 million cubic meters, evenly distributed between industrial wood and fuel wood.

In industrialized countries, 82% of the wood is not burned but is used for industrial purposes; in the less-developed countries 80% is used for fuel wood. Wood and other biomass fuels comprise 40–60% of the total energy resource for many developing Asian, Latin American, and African countries. Domestic cooking accounts for over 60% of the total national energy use in sub-Saharan Africa and exceeds 80% in several countries. In addition, some poor families spend 20% or more than 25% of their total household time collecting wood.

Biomass burned for cooking by the poor has been identified by the World Health Organization (WHO) as the major indoor air pollution health problem in the world today; WHO estimates that almost 1.5 billion people live in unhealthy air. High levels of wood smoke exposure—often 10 or more times the recommended WHO limits—have been reported in emission studies throughout developing countries. This, in turn, has been linked to acute respiratory infection (ARI), in particular pneumonia, along with a number of other aliments.

Women—who generally perform over 90% of domestic chores, including cooking—and their children make up the segment of the population most continuously exposed to indoor air pollution. As an example, one could mention that in a group of developing countries (India, Nepal, Nigeria, Kenya, Guatemala, and Papua New Guinea) typical exposure to suspended particulate matter (SPM) is 10–200 times higher than the WHO exposure guideline, while exposure to carbon monoxide is five times the limit and exposure to benzo[a]pyrene, a known cause of cancer, is at least 100 times that of the WHO guideline. The resulting pollution levels in homes and cooking huts in these countries is equivalent to the particulate dosage from smoking several packs of cigarettes a day. ARI is, in fact, the leading health hazard to children in developing countries and is responsible for an estimated 4.3 million deaths a year. Among all endemic diseases, including diarrhea, ARI is the most pervasive cause of chronic illness.

The living conditions that expose people to high levels of indoor air pollution have been well documented in Africa. The majority of sub-Saharan Africans live in rural areas. In Kenya, for example, only about 20% of the population lives in towns and cities. Family homes generally consist of small multipurpose buildings where the same room or few rooms are used for cooking, sleeping, and working. In many cases the total indoor volume is less than 40 m^3. In the extreme case of Masai homes in Kenya, indoor air volumes in the cooking area can be consistently less than 20 m^3. Also, rural cooking houses often have minimal ventilation.

Different fuel and stove combinations have widely different indoor levels of emissions, not only because stoves are more efficient and therefore take less time to cook but also because fuels are so different.

Which are the regional environmental problems?

These are pollution problems that often originate in cities but then spread over other geographical areas, frequently crossing national boundaries.

The main regional problems are as follows:

- Acid rain, causing a deposition of sulfuric (H_2SO_4) and nitric (HNO_3) acids and formed by the reaction of water (rain, snow, etc.) with SO_2 and NO_2. SO_2 originates in impurities present in fossil fuels and NO_2 is produced by the combustion of these fuels at high temperatures, leading to a combination of nitrogen and oxygen, both of which are part of the atmosphere.
- Pollution of seas and transboundary water bodies through oil leakages and other leakages in interstate or international waters. These leakages result in contamination of underground aquifers via the percolation of toxic substances. The sea is the ultimate sink for most of the liquid wastes and a considerable fraction of the solid wastes resulting from human activities on land. More than three-quarters of all marine pollution comes from land-based sources, through drainage and discharge into rivers, bays, and the open coast, and from the atmosphere. The remaining sources of marine pollution are shipping, dumping, and offshore mining and oil production, which are energy related.

What is acid rain?

Concerns about acidification damage were raised in Sweden more than 30 years ago, when the declining fish population in rivers and lakes appeared to be connected to changes in acidity of the water, as measured by an indicator named pH.

A pH of 7 is the neutral point, that is, the pH of pure water, which contains an equal number of positive and negative ions. Liquids with a pH below 7 are acid and those above 7 are nonacid, or basic. The pH of acid rain precipitation in the United States and Sweden is typically in the range of 4–5.

The two major acids in acid rain are sulfuric (H_2SO_4) and nitric (HNO_3). These acids are formed in the atmosphere from sulfur dioxide (SO_2) and oxides of nitrogen (NO_x). The products of fossil fuel combustion, SO_2 and NO_x, can be carried by wind to distances of up to 1,000 km from the point of emission. This causes acid rain far from the primary source of pollution, thus making it a regional problem, which frequently crosses national borders. SO_2 and NO_x cause damage through two mechanisms:

- Dry deposition, damaging vegetation and structure, or
- Wet deposition, when dissolved in rain, cloud water, or atmospheric water vapor.

The chemistry of the production process is only partly understood at present. It appears that a variety of mechanisms can cause acids to form and that the dominant chemical reactions depend on location and weather conditions as well as on the chemical composition of the local atmosphere. Sunlight, soot, and trace metals may also expedite the process of acid formation under certain circumstances.

There is a natural flux of S and N oxides due to volcanic emissions, biomass burning, lightning, and so on, but the natural flux, which is evenly spread out, does not give deposition fluxes higher than about 0.28 g of sulfur per square meter per year. What is really significant, however, is the flux of deposition of S or N of anthropogenic origin, because it is concentrated in a few industrial regions.

Which are the global environmental problems?

These are environmental problems that transcend national boundaries such as the emissions of carbon dioxide (CO_2) from fossil fuels burning and deforestation of native forests, and methane emissions (CH_4) and other gases responsible for the greenhouse effect.

Other global environmental problems indirectly related to energy include ozone emissions, deforestation for the production of fuel wood and charcoal as well as for agricultural expansion; accumulation of heavy metals (such as mercury, which is emitted by coal thermopower plants that then enters the food chain) in living organisms; human-made toxic compounds (such as PCBs—polychlorinated biphenyls) found in fluids used in electric equipment; and radioactive substances deriving from nuclear accidents, nuclear tests, and radioactive leakages.

What is the greenhouse gas effect?

The Earth's atmosphere is almost fully transparent to incident solar radiation. A fraction of this radiation is reflected to space, but most of it hits the planet surface, mainly as visible light, where it is absorbed and reemitted as thermal radiation. However, the atmosphere contains a small amount of gases, mainly carbon dioxide (CO_2), that are not transparent to thermal radiation and that act as a blanket, warming the whole atmosphere and the surface of the Earth in the same way as a farm greenhouse remains sufficiently warm in winter to allow the growth of out-of-season vegetables and flowers (Figure 8.1).

In 1896 Svente Arrhenius suggested that anthropogenic CO_2 emissions result in warming of the Earth, but this concept remained an academic issue until the mid-20th century.

The origin of this blanket is the burning or oxidation of organic matter, and it has remained approximately constant for the last few thousand years. However, since the beginning of the industrial age at the end of the 18th century, the burning of increased amounts of fossil fuels has resulted in the steady rise in the amount of CO_2 in the atmosphere.

As a consequence of the action of the so-called greenhouse gas effect, the planet emits less heat into space. The existence of the atmosphere and of the greenhouse gases allows life on the planet. They act as stabilizers against sudden changes in temperature between night and day. Without them it is

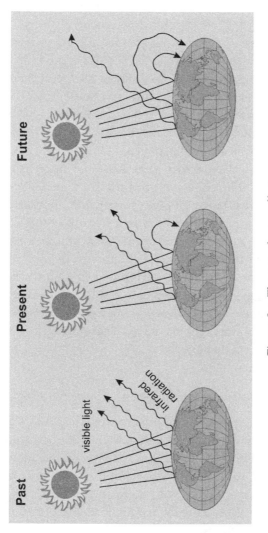

Figure 8.1 The greenhouse effect

estimated that the average temperature on the Earth's surface would be 15–20°C below zero. Whereas the Moon and Mars do not have an atmosphere and suffer from large differences in temperature, Venus has a very thick "cover" of carbon dioxide, keeping its temperature permanently high.

The degree of heating produced depends on the concentration and properties of each gas and on the amount of time during which the gases stay in the atmosphere.

Aerosols (small particles) from volcanoes, from industrial sulfate emission, and from other sources may absorb and reflect radiation as well. In most cases, aerosols tend to cool the climate. Aerosols and ozone (both tropospheric and strato-spheric) are also factors that cause an increase in the greenhouse effect; however, the effect is much smaller and scientific uncertainty is even larger. Moreover, there are changes in surface "albedo"—a reflectivity measure—altered, for example, by deforestation and other changes in land use. Any changes made by human beings in the radiant balance of the Earth, including those deriving from an increase in the amount of greenhouse gases or aerosols, will tend to change the atmosphere and ocean temperature, as well as the associated currents and types of climate. These changes overlap the natural climate changes.

What is the connection between global warming and energy?

The most relevant greenhouse gases are carbon dioxide, methane, nitrous oxide, and halons (chlorofluorocarbons and sulfur hexafluoride). Their concentrations in the atmosphere vary widely, from 383 parts per million in volume for CO_2 to 770 parts per billion in volume for methane. However, the effectiveness in blocking the reemission of heat from the Earth into the atmosphere depends on the characteristics of such gases. For example, one molecule of CH_4 is 21 times more effective than one molecule of CO_2 in blocking such emissions.

As a consequence, the contribution to global warming from different greenhouse gases in 2005 was the following: CO_2 contributed 76% (60% from fossil fuels use and 16% from deforestation), CH_4 contributed about 16%, N_2O about 6%, and the fluorinated gases contributed 2%.

In addition to that, the rate of emission of greenhouse gases is different for different gases: CO_2 emissions are increasing 0.4% per year, methane 0.8%/year, nitrous oxide 0.25%, and chlorofluorocarbons 4%/year. CO_2 originates mainly from the burning of fossil fuel, methane from the biological degradation of organic residues and waste (including animal and human wastes), and chlorofluorocarbons are gases used widely in hairsprays, refrigeration, and air conditioners.

The major carbon emitters (CO_2 and CH_4) for energy production are the industrialized countries (United States, Russia, Japan, Germany, Canada, United Kingdom, and a few others), but in developing countries (China, India, Brazil, Mexico, and others) emissions are growing rapidly. In addition, deforestation emissions and other forms of land-use change in developing countries are contributing significantly to the emissions.

The origin of CO_2 emissions from final end use is indicated in Table 8.1.

Table 8.1 The origin of CO_2 emissions

	Emissions of CO_2 in 2007 (%)
Electricity and heat	41
Transport	23
Industry	20
Residential	6
Other*	10
Total	100

*Others include commercial, public services, agriculture/forestry/fishing

What is the Intergovernmental Panel on Climate Change?

The Intergovernmental Panel on Climate Change (IPCC) is a scientific intergovernmental body tasked with reviewing and assessing the most recent scientific, technical, and socioeconomic information produced worldwide and relevant to the understanding of climate change. This panel was established in 1988 by the World Meteorological Organization (WMO) and the United Nations Environment Programme (UNEP), two organizations of the United Nations.

The IPCC does not carry out original research, nor does it do the work of monitoring climate or related phenomena. The IPCC assessment is based mainly on peer-reviewed and published scientific literature. A main activity of the IPCC is to prepare special reports on topics relevant to the implementation of the UN Framework Convention on Climate Change (UNFCCC).

The IPCC published its first report in 1990, its fourth in 2009; the fifth report is due in 2014.

The IPCC reports are the basis for policies adopted by the Conference of the Parties of the Climate Convention, which was adopted in 1992, and whose objective is to achieve stabilization of greenhouse gas concentrations in the atmosphere at a level that would prevent dangerous anthropogenic interference with the climate system (Article 2 of the Convention on Climate Change).

What are the facts concerning climate change?

The 11 years between 1995 and 2006 broke records in average temperature, as measured since 1850. Between 1906 and 2005, the Earth's average temperature increased 0.74°C. The increase in temperature per decade over the last 50 years nearly doubled that observed in the last 100 years. In the last century, the increase in average temperature in the Arctic doubled that of the planet's average.

Glaciers and mountain snow, as well as polar icecaps, decreased. In the Arctic, the spring defrost has increased by 15% since 1900. The dynamic defrosting effects contribute even more to the rise in ocean levels. The oceans absorb more than 80% of the heat incident on Earth and their average temperatures have increased to depths of up to 3,000 m, leading to a volumetric expansion and to an increase in sea level. The sea level rose 17 cm in the 20th century, at a rate of 1.8 mm a year in the period from 1961 to 2003 and 3.1 mm a year in the period from 1993 to 2003.

Rainfalls increased in the western regions of the Americas, Northern Europe, and North and Central Asia. Droughts increased in the Mediterranean, South Africa, and Sahel (between the Sahara Desert and the more fertile lands in the South) and parts of Southern Asia. There is evidence of increased cyclone activity, mainly in the North Atlantic. The increase in strong precipitation events is consistent with global warming and with the higher atmospheric concentration of water vapor. Intense and longer droughts have been more frequent since the 1970s, particularly in the tropics and subtropics. Also, associated with droughts are the alterations in ocean temperatures and wind standards and an increase in mountain defrosting.

Some of the increase in the number of extreme events is probably due to significant improvements in information access and to population growth. Extreme events are relatively rare and occur only 5% or less of the time. They are identified on the basis of the event's occurrence over time. On the basis of this definition the number of earthquakes per year has been approximately constant since 1960, but the number of cyclones has increased some 50% and the number of floods has increased 100% since 1995.

What are forecasts of climate models?

According to the IPCC modeling assessment, between 1999 and 2099, the average temperature of the planet will increase by 0.3 °C to 6.4 °C, the sea level will rise between 0.18 and 0.59 m, and the ocean pH will be reduced between 0.14 and 0.35.

The models also predict that warming will be greater on land than on oceans—and higher in the northern latitudes; perennial snow and ice will decrease; heat waves and strong precipitation will increase; cyclones will be more intense; extratropical storms will move toward the poles; and ocean currents will decrease by about 25%, altering the Gulf Stream—the consequence of which will be harsher winters in Western Europe.

Therefore, to stabilize the CO_2 concentrations in the atmosphere at 450 ppm, we will need to reduce emissions from fossil fuels by more than 50%. This will require a considerable effort.

Past and future CO_2 emissions caused by human activities will keep contributing to global warming and the increase in ocean levels for more than a millennium, owing to the time scale necessary to remove these gases from the atmosphere.

What are the environmental impacts from renewable sources?

Although environmental impacts resultant from energy use are usually directly linked to the use of fossil fuels, there are also problems that originate in the use of renewables, particularly if one evaluates the complete cycle, from "cradle to grave," of all the equipment and technology involved.

Because renewable sources presently make a modest contribution to the world's energy consumption, these problems will receive more attention as the contribution of renewables increases. The main impacts of the most important renewable sources are the following:

- Liquid effluent discharges and the use of fertilizers for modern biomass production contaminate groundwater aquifers with nitrates and other toxic substances and pose massive threats to fish and sea life in general.

- Wind equipment causes noise and aesthetic pollution and working blades pose a threat to migratory birds.
- Copper and lead found in the collectors and batteries used for solar energy result in the accumulation of toxic wastes in the environment.
- The reservoirs used for small hydro interfere with local fauna and flora and conflict with tourism.

What are the impacts of hydroelectricity plants?

Hydroelectricity plants, particularly the large ones, can seriously interfere with the environment because they require building large dams and the flooding of vast areas, changing water flows and blocking fish migration.

Flooding is an important indicator for the environmental impact caused by dams, but it is not the only one. Among other impacts are population removal (traditional native populations included); the alteration of river regimes downstream (which occurs after the dam has been built); sediment accumulation upstream; barriers to fish migration; proliferation of algae (eutrophication), water plants, and mosquitoes; extinction of endemic species; and loss of historical and archaeological heritages and tourism. Dam bursts are another possible risk. The impact of hydroelectricity enterprises can usually be estimated according to the power produced by hectare of reservoir. The larger this number, the lower the impact on the environment. A typical number for hydroelectric plants is 22 kW/hectare.

Hydroelectricity plants in operation do not produce CO_2 or other pollutants related to fossil fuels, with the exception of CH_4, which is produced by the decomposition of organic matter present in the reservoirs (especially if vegetation is not removed before flooding); however, construction and decommissioning of hydroelectricity plants results in CO_2 emissions.

How serious are oil leakages and spills?

An oil spill is a release of a liquid petroleum hydrocarbon into the environment due to human activity. The term often refers to marine oil spills, where oil is released into the ocean or coastal waters. Oil spills include releases of crude oil from tankers, offshore platforms, drilling rigs and wells, as well as spills of refined petroleum products (such as gasoline, diesel) and their by-products, heavier fuels used by large ships such as bunker fuel, or the spill of any oily refuse or waste oil. About half of the 30 billion barrels of oil consumed annually are transported by sea, where spills occur frequently. Oil pollution is a highly visible form of marine pollution and, therefore, has resulted in great public outcry and in resulting corrective measures. Average annual spillage from natural seeps and transportation is 9 million barrels, of which 1.8 million barrels are leaked in US waters.

The recent accident in deepwater exploration in the Gulf of Mexico highlighted the seriousness of the problem of oil spills. The Macondo well, was being drilled off the Louisiana coast by BP (British Petroleum) PLC using Transocean Ltd.'s Deepwater Horizon semisubmersible floating drilling rig. High pressure methane gas escaped, ignited and exploded engulfing the drilling rig and sank it, starting an oil spill of disastrous proportions. The spill amounted to 2.3 million barrels, according to BP estimates.

It was not the first of its kind in the Gulf of Mexico, and its environmental consequences were not more serious because much of the marine life in the area had been depleted over the centuries by pollution originating from the Mississippi River. The Ixtoc wildcat well blew out in mid-1979 while being drilled by Petroleos Mexicanos, resulting in what is now known as the second-largest spill in history. The Ixtoc blowout discharged an estimated 3.3 million barrels of oil into the Gulf until it was capped, nearly 10 months later, on March 23, 1980. Table 8.2 lists major oil spill disasters.

Table 8.2 Major oil spill disasters

	Gallons (millions)	Barrels (millions)
Gulf War 1991	1,000	24
Average annual spillage from natural spills and regular activities such as transportation	380	9
Ixtoc 1, 1979 (Mexico)	140	3.3
PB (Deepwater Horizon) 2010	97	2.3
Exxon Valdez, 1989	11	0.26

The Gulf War oil spill was initially estimated to be around 6 million barrels. However, according to a UN report, oil from other sources not included in the official estimates continued to pour into the Persian Gulf through June 1991 and may have reached 24 million barrels.

The Exxon Valdez spill in the Arctic in 1989 was a relatively modest spill of 260,000 barrels, but, owing to the ecological sensitiveness of that area, it provoked widespread coverage in the media and led to multibillion-dollar damage suits and a moratorium on oil drilling in that area.

Is deforestation caused by energy use?

The main reason for worldwide deforestation is changes in land use for the expansion of crops and grazing areas.

Deforestation and desertification are caused by a combination of intense human exploration and local ecological frailty. Such activities include population growth and migratory pressures; crop substitution; political problems, mainly in Africa, which hinder the seasonal migration of livestock breeders across provincial and national boundaries; poor policies promoting population relocation because of inappropriateness of soil and other conditions; and national development strategies that excessively prioritize predatory activities such as timber production, forest products, crops, and cattle raising. The latter two are the major causes of the Brazilian Amazon deforestation.

Even without government incentives, deforestation is a lucrative business: the market price of a hectare of virgin forest more than doubles after being burned and converted into pasture land. Additionally, the income derived from the timber can be very high. Some types of wood—such as mahogany—have high export market values. Forest plantations are increasing, but only account for 3.8% of the total world forest areas, or 140 million hectares. About 22% of the planted forests are used for water and soil conservation and 78% for productive ends, including energy.

The harvesting of fuel wood is not the major cause of deforestation or of the consequent desertification in developing countries. The exception occurs in sensitive areas, such as islands and elevated regions, where the vegetal cover is not enough to supply the energy needs of growing and needy populations.

Even though the use of fuel wood is not the main cause of deforestation, there are "hotspot" areas in the world in which its contribution to deforestation is of major importance. As previously discussed, this occurs mainly in Africa, where a large part of the population depends on fuel wood for cooking. Charcoal production can also cause the degradation of vast forest areas. This is the case in northern Thailand, which produces charcoal for Bangladesh. It is also the case in the states of northern Brazil, which produce charcoal to supply the steel industry. Many times the industry consumes "biomass waste" from sawmills, therefore being indirectly responsible for deforestation, a fact that still occurs in several charcoal works and metallurgy industries. Other industries that frequently use fuel wood without considering its origin are ceramics, gypsum, and food industries.

Besides desertification, deforestation significantly contributes to global warming due to CO_2 emission. Each hectare of tropical forest contains about 500 tons of stored CO_2, which goes into the atmosphere when the land is cleared.

What is the ecological footprint?

The ecological footprint is a measure of human demand on the Earth's ecosystems; it measures the amount of biologically productive land (measured in hectares) and sea area required to produce the resources consumed by human activity and absorb and render harmless the waste it generates.

Biologically productive land and sea include areas that (1) support human demand for food, fiber, timber, energy, and space for infrastructure and (2) absorb the waste products from the human economy (mainly CO_2). Biologically productive areas include cropland, forest, and fishing grounds but do not include deserts, glaciers, or the open ocean.

The "carbon footprint," which is often used as shorthand for the amount of carbon being emitted by an activity or organization, is an important contributor to the ecological footprint. The carbon component of the Ecological Footprint translates to the amount of productive land and sea area required to sequester carbon dioxide emissions. This is an indicator of the demand the burning of fossil fuels places on the planet.

There are several approaches to converting fossil fuel energy consumption into a corresponding land area. Each is based on a different rationale, but all produce approximately the same results: the annual per capita world consumption of 2 tons of oil equivalent (80 EJ) corresponds to the use of one hectare of ecologically productive land. One hectare is the size of a soccer field (or 10,000 m²).

Ethanol is a potentially renewable energy carrier that is technically and qualitatively equivalent to a fossil fuel. It is a homogeneous, concentrated fuel that can be stored and transported easily and can power human processes the same way fossil hydrocarbons do. For these reasons it is already being used in some places as a supplement to gasoline. The land area corresponding to fossil fuel consumption can therefore be represented as the productive land necessary to produce the equivalent amount of ethanol. This area comprises the amount of land needed to grow the plant material, usually sugarcane or corn, and the processing energy necessary to produce them.

Another method estimates the land area needed to sequester the CO_2 emitted from burning fossil fuel. The argument for this approach is that fossil carbon (in the form of CO_2) cannot be allowed to accumulate in the atmosphere if we wish to avoid possible climate change. If we continue to consume excessive quantities of fossil fuel, we have a responsibility to manage the waste products. This approach requires that we calculate the amount of "carbon sink" land require to assimilate the fossil CO_2 that we are injecting into the atmosphere.

Other contributions to the ecological footprint come from cropland, grazing land, fishing grounds, forest land, and built-up land.

According to the various ecological footprint calculations, humanity has already surpassed the capacity of the Earth to produce the resources needed and absorb the wastes it generates. The way to reverse this grim situation is to reduce dramatically fossil fuel consumption and adopt sustainable practices in other societal activities.

9

ENERGY COSTS

What are the costs of energy?

Energy costs across the world depend on a number of factors. Fossil fuels, which are commodities, are priced on the international market, but local conditions determine the costs of renewable energy. For example, wind-generated electricity can be produced at a cost of 4–8 cents/kWh. There is a factor of 2 between the cost of energy in the most favorable conditions and its cost in more problematic locations.

Table 9.1 lists indicative costs of electricity generation for all the renewable energy sources as well as nuclear, coal, and gas for comparison.

When comparing the cost of electricity generation from fossil fuels and nuclear fuel, one has to consider the investment costs and fuel costs, as well as the fact that plants burning fossil fuels emit CO_2. Such emissions are considered "externalities" and the cost of the damages they cause to human health and the environment are not included presently. This situation is likely to change and is changing already in some countries. The cost of externalities will probably be charged to producers as a carbon tax or charge. As a result, fossil fuels will become more expensive than others that do not emit CO_2, such as renewables and nuclear energy.

Table 9.1 The cost of electricity production

Technology	Energy cost ¢/kWh
Biomass energy	3–12
Wind electricity	4–8
Solar photovoltaic electricity	25–160
Solar thermal electricity	12–34
Low-temperature solar heat	2–25
Hydro energy	
Large	2–10
Small	2–12
Geothermal energy	2–10
Marine energy	
Tidal	8–15
Wave	10–30
Tidal stream/current	10–25
OTEC[a]	15–40
Nuclear	8.4
Coal	6.2
Coal (with CO_2 charge)	8.3
Gas	4.2–8.7
Gas (with CO_2 charge)	5.1–9.6

[a] Ocean Thermal Energy Conversion.

What are externalities?

Externalities are defined as costs of market transactions that are not captured in traditional energy costs, and they can be positive or negative. A negative externality is one that creates side effects that could be harmful to either the general public directly or through the environment, such as pollution generated from the burning of fossil fuels. A positive externality, on the other hand, is a benefit that extends beyond those directly initiating the activity, such as the development of a public park.

Arthur Pigou, a British economist best known for his work in welfare economics, argued that the existence of externalities justifies government intervention through legislation or regulation. "Pigovian taxation" philosophy promotes taxation of negative externalities, which are, essentially, activities associated with detrimental impacts. The Pigovian tax therefore shifts the emphasis from the subsidization of negative externalities to the subsidization of positive externalities, or activities that create benefits in order to further positively incentivize associated activities.

One of the most efficient solutions to externalities is to include them in the cost to those engaged in the activity, that is, to internalize the externality. This would keep externalities from being seen as market failures, which could, in turn, weaken the case for government intervention. It is generally believed that this approach is better than regulations.

Another method for controlling negative externalities associated with energy production is the "Cap and Trade" system. The Cap and Trade system sets maximum emission levels for a given group of sources over a specific time period. Unused allowances can be traded, bought and sold, or banked for future use. Over time, the cap is lowered and, in theory, this should encourage more efficient processes so that additional profits can be realized by selling allowances to less efficient producers.

In the 1990s, the European Union (EU) Commission launched ExternE, a major research program to provide a scientific basis for the quantification of energy-related externalities and to give guidance supporting the design of internalization measures. The program used a bottom-up impact pathway ranging from single-source emission via changes in air, soil, and water quality, to physical impacts such as increased emissions.

The ExternE study found that externalities in the European Union region ranged from 40 billion euro to 70 billion euro for fossil fuel and nuclear in 2003. The study highlighted that, if included in energy prices, identified externalities would double the cost of producing electricity from coal or oil and increase the cost of electricity production from gas by 30%.

A typical example of an externality would be a carbon charge on the cost of electricity generated in thermopower plants using fossil fuels. These charges will probably amount to US$25 per ton of CO_2 emitted, and they could increase the cost of coal-generated electricity by 2.1 ¢/kWh (from 6.2 to 8.3 ¢/kWh) and the cost of gas-generated electricity by 1¢/kWh. For the European Union, costs of externalities incurred from biomass, hydro, photovoltaic, and wind energies are generally smaller.

What are "learning curves"?

The environmental advantages of renewable technologies are well known, but, as with most new technologies, their cost is higher than conventional technologies based on fossil fuels.

For example, electricity generated from coal, which is the most important source of electricity around the world, is estimated to be 6.2 ¢/kWh, while solar photovoltaic electricity is estimated to be in the range of 25–160 ¢/kWh (Table 9.1). This is not an unusual situation and most of the products used today such as automobiles—which are quite accessible to many people—were very expensive 100 years ago, when they were first introduced. Mass production with economies of scale and technological learning has lowered the cost of automobiles considerably.

Accelerating the development of new technologies is particularly relevant for the widespread adoption of renewable energies, which is fundamental for environmental sustainability. The "market penetration" of a particular energy source is the result of a complex combination of factors such as the availability of competing energy sources, the convenience of their use, and their cost. Usually, prices decrease as sales increase, owing to economies of scale, and "learning curves."

An indicator called "progression ratio" (PR) measures the decrease in cost of a given technology as production increases. Typically, a PR of 80% means that the cost decreases by 20% every time production doubles. The smaller the PR, the faster the costs decrease.

In the initial phase of the introduction of new technologies, subsidies might be needed until increases in production lead to lower costs. Such subsidies generate distortions in the market in the long run, and, therefore, they must be progressively eliminated, as the fostered technology reaches maturity.

How large are energy subsidies?

Policy makers usually justify energy subsidies with the argument that they contribute to economic growth, poverty reduction, and enhance security of energy supply. It is indeed true that judicious use of energy subsidies can help address market failures or respond to social and distributional objectives, especially where social welfare mechanisms for directly providing income support to the poor do not exist. Subsidies can be critical for ensuring access to modern energy services, including electricity. In addition, well-designed and targeted subsidies can overcome market failures by mitigating environmental problems in specific contexts, for example, by encouraging alternatives to biomass in areas where deforestation is an issue.

However, energy subsidies can put societies onto inefficient consumption and production paths. Fossil-fuel subsidies to consumers can create dependencies and discourage users from shifting to cleaner sources of energy. Similarly, subsidies to specific energy technologies undermine the development and commercialization of other technologies that might ultimately become more economically (as well as environmentally) attractive. As such, subsidies can "lock-in" technologies to the exclusion of other, more promising ones.

The IEA estimates that fossil-fuel-related consumption subsidies amounted to US$557 billion in 2008. Analysis shows that, if these subsidies were phased out by 2020, it would result in a reduction in primary energy demand at the global level of 5.8% and a fall in energy-related carbon-dioxide emissions of 6.9%, compared with a baseline in which subsidy rates remain unchanged.

The total order of magnitude of subsidies to fossil fuels, both to consumers and producers—almost US$700 billion a year—is roughly equivalent to 1% of world GDP.

To put these estimates into perspective, estimated agriculture subsidies in OECD countries were close to US$400 billion in 2008.

On the other hand, the Global Subsidies Initiative (GSI) estimates that around US$100 billion per year is spent to subsidize alternatives to fossil fuels, mainly in Germany, Spain, Japan, and the United States.

PART IV

TECHNICAL SOLUTIONS AND POLICIES

10

ENERGY EFFICIENCY

What are the existing technical solutions to the present energy system?

Existing technical solutions to the present energy system include higher efficiency, increased reliance on renewable sources, deployment of new energy technologies, and policies to accelerate the adoption of new technologies.

These solutions are complementary, because it is possible to develop a new technology for obtaining renewable energy with simultaneous gains in efficiency. In this sense solar energy offers great possibilities. A more efficient energy use must be made whenever possible, as this extends the life of the finite sources of fossil fuels, reduces environmental impacts, and, in general, offers economic advantages in terms of investment returns.

What is the potential of energy efficiency?

There is a long way between the theoretical potential of an energy source, its technical, economic and market potential:

- *The theoretical potential* represents what may be achieved on the basis of physical laws—particularly the laws of thermodynamics—and the existing natural resources.

- *The technical potential* represents energy savings resulting from reduction of friction and other losses as well as the use of more efficient technologies. The technical potential does not take economic considerations into account.
- *The economic potential* is achievable in ideal open market economies where there is competition among investors and availability of information among all users for decision making. In an ideal open market there is no government interference in administering prices.
- *The market potential* is what is expected to be obtained given the commercial conditions. Such conditions are determined by market barriers and imperfections such as government interference and lack of information between agents who sell and buy publicly. The market potential is also determined by social barriers in which externalities such as ecologic problems and health impacts are taken into account.

What are the advantages of energy efficiency?

The 20th century's energy system evolved at a time when energy (mainly fossil fuels) was sufficiently cheap and abundant that the economic penalty for saving energy was not worth the effort, economically. Before the oil crisis, expenditures on energy in most industries amounted to less than a few percent. After the oil crisis, when the cost of oil quadrupled, a great effort was made to improve the efficiency of energy use both from the "supply side," that is, in the conversion process of primary energy sources to electricity and on the "end-use side," that is, the equipment using the electricity or fuels, such as refrigerators, lighting apparatuses, or automobiles.

The advantages of improved energy efficiency are reduced use of fossil fuels and an increased security of supply, because less energy is needed to perform the same tasks. There is also a reduction in environmental impacts.

Opportunities for reduced energy consumption exist in all steps of the energy chain, and they are particularly important in the conversion of primary sources of energy to energy services in residential, industrial, transportation, public, and commercial sectors, as each of these sectors makes demands along the energy chain. Reductions of more than 40% could be cost-effective and achievable in the former Soviet Union (and other transition economies) within the next two decades as old and inefficient technologies are replaced. In most developing countries—the cost-effective improvement potential ranges from 30% to more than 45% owing to the fact that most of the industrial machinery in use was imported from industrialized countries in the past and is thus inefficient.

The implied improvements of about 2% per year could be enhanced through structural changes in industrialized and transitional countries, shifts toward services and less energy-intensive industrial production, and saturation effects in the residential and transportation sectors (that is, there is a limit to the number of cars, refrigerators, television sets, etc., that a society can absorb). Structural changes can come from increased recycling and substitution of energy-intensive materials, improved material efficiency, and intensified use of durable and investment goods. The combined result of structural changes and efficiency improvements could accelerate the annual decline in energy intensity to perhaps 2.5%. How much of this potential will be realized depends on the effectiveness of policy frameworks and measures, the changes in attitude and behavior, and the level of entrepreneurial activity in energy conservation and material efficiency.

What are the barriers to energy efficiency?

Energy efficiency or energy conservation is a component of economic efficiency, but not always the dominant one. The productive sector simply considers energy as a relatively minor production ingredient, in addition to capital, labor, and raw materials.

In addition, issues related to energy frequently require specific knowledge that is quite distant from the enterprise's final activity. The situation gets even more difficult when the income of a company, of an economic sector, and even of a country, derives mainly from selling primary energy products. In these cases, there is opposition to energy conservation, as efficiency measures represent, at least in principle, a decrease in profits. That is the case, for example, of manufacturers of vehicles for the luxury segment; power utilities, which sell electricity for profit (except for sectors with subsidized prices, such as for low-income populations); large oil companies; and international bodies, such as the Organization of Petroleum Exporting Countries (OPEC).

The main barriers to energy conservation, in addition to the loss of income on the part of the utilities, are the low price of energy for certain sectors, which does not reflect fully the generation costs; the lack of priority placed upon energy, as it is considered a fixed cost in companies devoted to other activities; lack of consumer understanding about transitioning to a more efficient system, as long-term costs are not evident; the lack of information provided by manufacturers and by sellers of products that consume energy; the limited availability of efficient equipment in the market; the lack of financing by third parties; the short-term economic-financial view, mainly in inflationary cultures with high interest rates; and the lack of laws and regulatory instruments that make energy efficiency compulsory.

What is the potential for energy efficiency in power production?

The maximum efficiency of conventional systems for electricity generation (steam turbines and boilers) using fossil fuels is rarely greater than 35%, which means that 65% of energy available in the fossil fuels is dissipated as low-temperature heat. Modern turbines, however, usually recover lost heat, using the residual heat to generate more electricity and increasing their efficiency to approximately 50%. Such systems are called combined cycle systems.

Owing to the introduction of these systems, between 1990 and 2007, the efficiency of thermal electricity generation with natural gas increased from 34% to 42% on average. Coal electricity generation did not benefit from these gains and efficiency stayed practically constant because the equipment in use in most developing countries has not been modernized. For oil, efficiency has likewise stayed practically constant.

Chinese and Indian plants using coal are the least efficient with efficiencies around 20%. By comparison, Japan's thermo-power plants had already achieved a 36% average efficiency by 1965. By 2004, Japanese thermopower plants had reached an average efficiency of 40% and some of its units had efficiencies of up to 52%. Denmark had a 36% average efficiency in 1960 and 52% in 2000.

What is the potential of energy efficiency in buildings?

Energy in buildings is required in two ways:

Operating energy (usually called direct) is the energy needed to operate the services and amenities in buildings, including thermal comfort, refrigeration, illumination, communication and entertainment, sanitation, and others. The cost of operating energy ends up in the monthly bill for energy services.

Embodied energy (usually called indirect) is the energy needed for the production and transportation of the materials used in construction, the manufacturing of furniture and appliances, and the provision of infrastructure services such as water and sanitation. Embodied energy is highly dependent on the design and construction technique of buildings.

One can try to make buildings more efficient either by investing more in the construction phase to reduce the embodied energy or by investing heavily in more efficient appliances to reduce other energy consumption in the operation of the building. Over a 50-year life-cycle direct energy in the OECD building sector accounts for 84% of the energy used in OECD countries which means that in each year as much as 15% of the sunk energy is consumed in the operation of the building. This amount is even higher in some industrialized countries and lower in developing countries.

In the European Union space heating accounts for the single largest use of energy. Buildings account for up to two-thirds of total energy use in the cold regions of China and in the former Soviet Union. Lighting sometimes accounts for the largest single use of electricity in commercial buildings, although in hot climates, air conditioning tends to be the single largest use of electricity.

In buildings, approaches that optimize individual component efficiencies typically result in 20–30% efficiency gains in heating and cooling energy use, while novel approaches focusing on holistic methods using integrated design principles have been demonstrated to achieve as much as 60–90% energy savings compared with standard practices.

Passive houses that reduce energy use for heating and cooling by 90% or more are already found in many European countries. What makes them "passive" is the fact that very little external energy is used to heat the house in the winter or to cool it in the summer. Increased investments in building insulation are partly offset by lower investments in heating and cooling systems, as energy costs for operation are almost eliminated, making these new options very attractive.

Buildings in developing countries do not usually require ambient heating or hot water, thus saving significant amounts of energy and costs. In addition, by using almost exclusively local materials, production costs can be reduced—such as occurs in India with low-cost bricks.

How can we increase energy efficiency in buildings?

Approximately 40% of all energy used today is spent on building construction and use. Selected energy efficient technologies and practices for buildings are as follows:

Building envelopes	Energy-efficient windows, insulation (walls, roof, floor), reduced air infiltration
Space conditioning	Air conditioner efficiency measures (e.g., thermal insulation, improved heat exchangers, advanced refrigerants, more efficient motors) Centrifugal compressors, efficient fans and pumps, and variable air volume systems for large commercial buildings
Appliances	Advanced compressors, evacuated panel insulation (refrigerators), washing machines and dryers with higher spin speeds
Cooking	Improved efficiency biomass stoves, efficient gas stoves (ignition, burners)
Lighting	Compact fluorescent lamps, improved phosphors, solid-state electronic ballast technology, advanced lighting control systems (including day-lighting and occupancy sensors), and task lighting
Motors	Variable speed drives. Size optimization. Improvement of power quality
Other	Building energy management systems, passive solar use (building design), solar water heaters

Legal standards (e.g., building codes; well-informed consumers, planners, and decision makers; motivated operators; market-based incentives such as certificate markets; and an adequate payments system for energy) are central to the successful implementation of energy efficiency improvements.

North American refrigerators provide one example of the gains possible in energy efficiency. Despite the fact that the size of refrigerators has tripled over the past 50 years, they use much less power and cost less. In the period 1947–2002 refrigerator size increased from less than 400 to 1800 ft^3, while the average price dropped two-thirds between 1975 and 2000. Energy use per unit increased from 400 to 1800 kWh/yr in the period 1947–1975, and then dropped by up to 462 kWh/yr by the year 2000.

This was achieved through the use of better insulating materials that minimize heat losses.

What is building retrofitting?

In industrialized countries, where the problem of providing houses to the great majority of the population has been achieved, the main housing task is to retrofit existing buildings to save energy. Considerable energy savings can be obtained in this process. Besides stricter building codes for new buildings and maintenance requirements for the existing ones, energy certificates are required and financial incentives (such as tax reduction and financing) are granted to more efficient technologies. With these measures, Switzerland achieved a 50% energy savings in commercial buildings over a 20-year period.

Developing countries face the problem of a huge housing deficiency, so the opportunities exist in improvements to building construction methods. Experience shows that the cost of producing more-efficient buildings is not much higher than that of conventional ones. The move toward efficient building construction can be accelerated through building codes and standards.

Illustrative model simulations for an "artificial" city suggest improvement potentials of at least a factor of 2 if more energy-efficient buildings and more compact urban forms (at least medium density and mixed use layouts) are enacted. Also implicated in such a simulation is energy systems optimization through distributed generation and resulting cogeneration of electricity, heat, and air conditioning (adding another 10–15% improvement in efficiency in urban energy use). Cogeneration is discussed in Chapter 11.

What is the impact of urbanization on energy use?

Urbanization is increasing dramatically in Brazil, China, India, and other countries in which the bulk of new construction is taking place in the commercial sector. In India projected growth of the commercial building sector is 7% per year. Its built area currently totals only 200 million m^2, but, by 2030, it is expected that 869 million m^2 of additional space of commercial buildings will be constructed in its cities.

About 70% of the world's energy is consumed in cities, even though only approximately one-half of the world's population lives in cities. In most developing countries, particularly in China, city residents use almost twice as much energy as the national average due to higher income. In the United States and the European Union, where income is more evenly distributed, energy consumption in cities is slightly lower than the national average because suburbs and rural areas are wealthier, houses are larger, and car and trucks are used more than in cities.

In urban areas, systemic characteristics are generally more important determinants of energy use efficiency than the characteristics of individual consumers or technological artifacts. For instance, the share of high occupancy public and/or nonmotorized transport modes in urban transit is a more important determinant of urban-transport-energy use than the efficiency of the vehicle fleet.

Incremental tightening of building codes and building standards and specifications is an essential factor in driving building construction and even cities more generally toward a more sustainable direction. There is, however, the risk of a "lock-in" in obsolete technologies and concepts. It is essential therefore that building codes be dynamic in nature, continuously adopting state-of-the-art efficiency levels.

What is the energy efficiency potential in industry?

In global terms, industry accounts for about 35% of power consumption and has a 25% potential for efficiency gains, 30% of which is possible in engine efficiency.

There are several "horizontal technologies," such as components, which are common to many industrial areas. Examples are engines, gears, compressors, boilers, membranes for separation of substances, laser processors for cutting and perforation of steel, as well as solar heating for refrigeration and air conditioning.

There are also "specialized technologies" for the production of steel, chemical products, nonferrous metals (such as aluminum and zinc), paper and pulp, and food and beverages. Such technologies, for example, packaging of goods or water purification for the production of beer, are very specific and are not applicable across the board.

Usually industries in developing countries (such as China) do not perform as well as similar industries in the OECD. But even the best performing practices are still worse than the best methods available. For example, in ammonium production the energy intensity in China is 39–65 and in the OECD it is 33–44, while the best available practice is 19.1. Energy intensity in this context is the energy spent for each unit of product, usually measured in kilogram of oil equivalent for kilogram of product.

In different industrial sectors, adopting the best achievable technology can result in savings of 10–30% below the current average. The payback period for these measures ranges from less than 9 months to 4 years. A systematic analysis of materials and energy flows indicates significant potential for process integration, heat pumps, and cogeneration; for example, savings of 30% are seen in dairy, chocolate, ammonia, and vinyl chloride.

Energy management standards from the International Organization for Standardization (ISO) are likely to be effective in facilitating industrial end-use efficiency. Effective management of the demand side can be facilitated by a combination of mandated measures and market strategies. ISO is an international organization based in Geneva and founded in 1947. It is the world's largest developer and publisher of international standards, networking 170 countries and approving international norms in all technical areas.

What is the energy efficiency potential in transportation?

The transportation sector as a whole was responsible for 27% of the world's energy consumption in 2008 (up from 23% in 1971). For the OECD it was 33% in 2008 (up from 24% in 1971). For non-OECD countries it was 18% in 2008 (up from 13% in 1971).

Increased mechanical efficiency (currently 40%) could be achieved by decreasing the power required of the engine. This can be done by reducing air drag, rolling resistance, weight, friction in the transmission gears, and vehicle accessory loads. Increasing the actual average mechanical efficiency to approximately 65% percent seems an achievable goal. In contrast, thermal efficiency is limited by the laws of thermodynamics to less than 40%.

The mechanical efficiency of typical US automobiles is roughly 35%, on average, for urban driving and about 50% for highway driving. The overall mechanical efficiency averages about 40%. It is lower for high-powered automobiles and higher for low-powered automobiles.

Improving mechanical efficiency at a given load requires that the power necessary to operate the engine be reduced, particularly the energy used for pumping, overcoming friction, and driving engine accessories. There are many strategies for achieving this: engine size, sources of friction themselves, and engine speed. The Otto spark ignition gasoline engines in use today have a low cost and high power-to-weight ratio and are, therefore, difficult to replace with other types of engines.

Working against improvements in the present transportation system is the fact that advances in designing better automobile engines and vehicles to guarantee higher energy efficiency are inhibited by other factors of customer acceptance. These include visual attractiveness, safety, capacity, performance, and comfort (even luxury). Safety is also one of the key features that must be taken into account in energy-efficient designs, and it has been repeatedly argued that smaller and more efficient automobiles increase highway fatalities.

For such reasons, the maximum power of new automobiles has increased in recent years: the average new-automobile power/weight ratio has risen from a low 70 HP/1,000 kg to 90 HP/1,000 kg, although high power is only required in unusual driving conditions such as acceleration at high speed and on mountainous roads. Some governments have tried to counteract such trends by imposing taxes on gas suppliers, but manufacturers have systematically opposed such taxes by adopting the strategy of improving fuel economy rather than paying even a small "gas-guzzler" tax.

Developing countries present some special problems in improving the efficiency of their transportation systems. In many countries the leading world automotive manufacturers, including General Motors, Chevrolet, Renault, Volkswagen, Fiat, Mercedes Benz, and Scania, have established subsidiaries where cars and trucks are either assembled or entirely locally built. The cars are basically the same as the ones produced in the manufacturers' home countries. Despite this, these cars and trucks generally have fuel efficiencies that are 20–50% lower than their counterparts in industrialized countries, mainly because of bad maintenance practices, low-quality fuels, and poor roads.

In the maritime sector, a combination of technical measures to apply state-of-the-art knowledge to hull and propeller design and maintenance could reduce energy consumption by 4–20% in older ships and 5–30% in new ships. Reducing the speed at which a ship operates leads to a significant benefit of reduced energy consumption. For example, a reduction in a ship's speed from 26 knots to 23 knots can yield a 30% fuel saving. The knot is equal to one nautical mile (1.852 km) per hour, approximately 1.151 mile per hour.

What is the "rebound" effect?

In the short run, at the consumer level, energy conservation efforts are clearly financially rewarding; similarly, industries producing energy-intensive products can increase profits considerably by reducing energy consumption.

However, savings in energy consumption can lead to additional activity through either greater use of the same product or movement toward another energy-using action, that is, it can generate a "rebound" effect. For example, as a *direct rebound effect*, a car owner might drive a more-efficient automobile further than a less-efficient one. An *indirect rebound effect* might be that a consumer uses the money saved on a more-efficient automobile to buy another car. Similar effects occur for energy consumed in buildings. There are also *economy-wide effects*, whereby new technologies create new production possibilities and increase economic growth.

There are many studies on the subject and and the magnitude of the rebound effect varies from 0 to 50%, depending on the sector. Typical numbers for space heating are 10–30%; for space cooling, 0–50%; for lighting, 5–20%; for water heating, 10–40%; and for residential lighting, 5–12%.

For automobiles a 10% improvement in efficiency leads to an average 2% increase in distance traveled. For appliances (or "white goods") indirect effects have led to a 90% rebound effect in purchases of large units with more features, according to some studies. These percentages do not reflect economy-wide effects.

The rebound effect of savings obtained through energy efficiency might not be enough to reduce increases in overall consumption in a society with an increasing population and rising incomes. In this case gains in efficiency will still be offset by an increase in energy consumption and carbon emissions.

11

NEW TECHNOLOGIES

What is cogeneration?

Cogeneration or CHP (combined heat and power) devices allow the simultaneous production of electric and thermal energy in energy systems. They typically recover and use waste heat from a thermal power plant burning coal.

These systems are widely used in Eastern Europe to distribute hot water (at temperatures between 80 and 150 °C) to houses and apartments, and even to whole districts using heat generated in a central station. Thus, these systems are called "district heating." Heat at moderate temperatures can also be used in absorption chillers for cooling. A plant producing electricity, heat, and gas is called a trigeneration or polygeneration plant.

Eleven percent of the electricity generation in the European Union uses cogeneration, but there are large differences between member states ranging from 2 to 60%.

In Brazil, cogeneration is used widely in industrial installation using sugarcane bagasse, which is produced after the cane juice has been extracted and converted into either sugar or ethanol. The bagasse is solid biofuel that can be burned to produce all the heat and electricity needed in the industrial process of sugar or ethanol production. In modern efficient installations surplus, bagasse is used to produce electricity to be sold to the electricity grid.

What is the role of new technologies for fossil fuels?

There is a technological revolution currently under way in power generation, where advanced systems are replacing steam turbine technologies. Natural gas- fired combined cycle plants offer low cost, high efficiency, and low environmental impact, and they are being utilized wherever natural gas is readily available. In some countries they are even replacing new large hydropower projects. Cogeneration (i.e., the combined delivery of heat and power or CHP) based on gas turbines and combined cycles is more cost effective and can play a much larger role in the energy economy than cogeneration with steam turbines, because combined cycles make use of waste heat while steam turbines do not. Reciprocating engines and emerging microturbine and fuel-cell technologies are also strong technologies for cogeneration on smaller scales, including commercial and apartment buildings. Coal gasification by partial oxidation with oxygen to make synthetic gases (mainly carbon oxide and hydrogen), usually called "syngas," makes it possible to produce electricity via integrated gasifier combined cycle plants, at high efficiencies and with air pollutant emissions nearly as low as for natural gas combined cycles. These plants are branded integrated gasifier combined cycle (IGCC). Today, power from IGCC cogeneration plants would often be competitive with power from coal or steam electric plants in either cogeneration or power-only configurations.

Very clean syngas-derived synthetic fuels such as synthetic middle distillates and dimethyl ether can soon play significant roles by supplementing conventional liquid fuels (for transportation, cooking, peak power generation, etc.). They can alleviate oil supply security concerns and facilitate the implementation of tougher air pollution regulations. Such fuels can often be produced for global markets at competitive cost from huge low-cost natural gas supplies that would otherwise be stranded assets at remote sites. In natural gas-poor, coal-rich regions, a promising strategy for producing such fuels is via coal gasification and "polygeneration"—the coproduction of various combinations of clean fuels, chemicals, and electricity.

Such systems might include production of extra syngas for distribution, by pipelines, to small-scale cogeneration systems in factories and buildings, thereby enabling clean and efficient use of coal on small as well as large scales. Rapidly growing polygeneration activity is already under way in several countries based on gasification of low-quality petroleum feedstocks.

What is Carbon Capture and Storage?

Carbon Capture and Storage (CCS) is a technology to capture the CO_2 gases emitted from power stations and bury them into the ground at high pressures, either in depleted gas, oil, or coal deposits, naturally occurring caverns, saline aquifers, or the deep ocean. If no leaking occurs, these could be considered permanent reservoirs.

Such technology has been used in the past for enhanced oil recovery, in which CO_2 is pumped into reservoirs to bring to the surface oil that would not naturally gush out. There are almost 40 years of experience in enhanced oil recovery (EOR), and presently approximately 40 million tons of CO_2 are being used for this purpose.

About one-third of all the CO_2 emissions from fossil-fuel-based energy sources are from thermopower plants. The idea of capturing CO_2 from the gases exhausted from power plant stacks did not originate from concerns over the greenhouse effect, but as a possible source of commercial carbon gas (for example, as used by beverage and dry ice industries). Several such CO_2 recovery plants were built and operated in the United States, but most of them failed economically and were closed when the price of crude oil fell in the 1980s.

Once CO_2 is captured, the problem is removing it. Its commercial use is extremely limited, and thus there is no economic incentive for capturing large amounts of CO_2. Apart from this, there is the risk of CO_2 leaking back into the atmosphere. In high concentrations, CO_2 is toxic and may cause deaths, as occurred in the Republic of Cameroon in 1986, when CO_2 leakage from volcanic origin in Lake Nyos killed over 1,700 people as well as livestock and wild animals. CO_2 capture processes usually require a large amount of energy, reducing the conversion efficiency of the plant and the available power—and thus increasing the amount of CO_2 produced per power unit generated.

Although CCS technology is usually linked to coal and natural gas thermopower plants, nothing prevents it from being applied to biomass power generation (as in the case of sugarcane bagasse). In this case, the CO_2 liquid emissions would be negative, as the carbon in the atmosphere is synthesized in the plants, transformed into energy, and injected underground.

Finding adequate reservoirs for CO_2 storage is not a trivial problem and in practice might present great difficulties. One possibility would be to transport the CO_2 from the source to its final deposition, be it through a gas duct network (which would cause problems with land owners and ecologically sensitive areas) or by road or railway transportation (which would overload the transportation infrastructure and require more energy).

The cost of capturing and storing CO_2 from thermal electricity-generating power plants using coal is appreciable. Although few pilot plant projects are in operation today, estimates exist that the cost of electricity for the operation of industrial-scale CCS projects would rise by at least 50–100%. Considering full life-cycle emissions, CCS technology can reduce CO_2 emissions from fossil fuel combustion from stationary sources by about 65–85%. The costs of capturing and storing CO_2 are estimated to be in the range of US\$30 to over US\$200 per ton of CO_2, depending on the availability of adequate places for storage and the characteristics of such places. If it becomes necessary to transport the CO_2 through pipes over long distances, costs will climb upward.

What is the future of transportation?

An increase in the use of cars seems to be inevitable, but excessive use is a problem—and not a solution—for urban mobility.

There are now almost 1 billion automobiles circulating in the world, but vehicle ownership per 1,000 persons varies widely. In the United States there are almost 800 cars per 1,000 people, while in the OECD, the number is approximately 500 cars per 1,000 people. If the use of cars in developing countries, currently around 100 cars per 1,000 people, reaches OECD or US levels, problems related to the environment, infrastructure, and land use will become insoluble.

From the view point of social organization the best solution to urban mobility is public transportation. Bus corridors and traffic management are relatively cheap and fast solutions. Nonmotorized transportation can be stimulated within neighborhoods and communities.

From the view point of technology the future of transportation hinges on improvements in the efficiency of current motors and a shift toward electric motors, with a transitional period of hybrids. Biofuels also offer a possible—albeit partial—solution to the problem of replacing fossil fuels.

Are natural gas, liquefied petroleum gas, and hydrogen alternatives for transportation?

Natural gas is one of the fuel alternatives and, compared to gasoline, its use may achieve up to a 70% reduction in CO_2 emissions and eliminate particulate matter and SO_x emissions. Both liquefied petroleum gas (LPG) and compressed natural gas (CNG) have a higher hydrogen–carbon ratio than gasoline and, therefore, emit less CO_2 per energy unit. Moreover, their higher octane rates allow their use under higher compression. Although significant changes in engine design are not needed to allow the use of LPG or CNG, it is necessary to take precautions to prevent NO_x and hydrocarbon emissions from increasing considerably due to inadequate conversions.

Hydrogen is also an important energy carrier and can be used for ultra-low-emission vehicles. Hydrogen storage is a problem due to its low-energy density. The use of compressed hydrogen is the most viable form, although it is also possible to store liquid hydrogen or use metallic hydrates. Hydrogen-based fuel cells are also under research and development. Even though proponents state that hydrogen is not more dangerous than gasoline if properly handled, hydrogen is a very explosive gas and, therefore, safety problems have to be solved before it gains public acceptance.

Concerning its compatibility with the existing infrastructure (production, storage, and distribution), hydrogen would need very significant changes. At present, the most likely hydrogen source is natural gas. Coal producers also have great interest in the hydrogen economy, although, in the future, hydrogen could be produced from biomass, a renewable resource.

Are electrically powered vehicles feasible?

Electrical vehicles that use batteries are of great interest nowadays, especially for urban environments. If the electricity moving them comes from a non-fossil source, their use could result in a significant reduction in the emission of greenhouse gases. The main hindrance to their wide implementation is the present state of chemical batteries technology, resulting in high-cost, heavy vehicles with limited range. Furthermore, whereas a gasoline automobile can be fueled in a few minutes, the battery recharge for electric cars usually requires several hours. Large-scale introduction of electric vehicles would require great changes in infrastructure, not only in the power distribution system and in the automobiles but also in the power generation industry.

Hybrid vehicles run on a combination of batteries, which energize the propulsion system, and a small internal combustion engine fueled by gasoline, diesel oil, or biofuels, which recharges the batteries. Regenerative breaking also helps in recharging the batteries. Lighter and long-lasting lithium-ion batteries for automobiles are being developed to replace traditional lead-acid batteries.

With hybrid vehicles, a fuel economy of up to 50% and a reduction in emissions of about 70% can be achieved. The great advantage of this technology is that the small gasoline-fueled engine works at a constant rotation and speed, saving fuel and reducing pollution and noise levels. Hybrid vehicles can reach up to 40% efficiency (30 km or 18.64 miles/liter).

Hybrid electric vehicles (HEVs) offer lower emissions and better fuel economy, 30–50% higher than in comparable conventional vehicles. Plug-in hybrid electric vehicles (PHEVs) are the next step, potentially offering zero-emission transportation, depending on the vehicle driving range. All-electric or battery electric vehicles (BEVs) with high efficiency but low driving range and short battery life have limited market penetration at present. Increasing the performance of high-energy batteries for PHEVs could lead to the higher market penetration of BEVs. The problem remains, of course, of generating electricity to charge the batteries; if this electricity originates in fossil-fuel-generating plants, BEV usage will not achieve much more than transferring the source of emissions from the vehicles (automobiles or trucks) to the electricity generating plants.

What are fuel cells?

Fuel batteries or fuel cells produce energy by electrochemical means, as opposed to the combustion processes in conventional engines. Hydrogen reacts chemically with oxygen, forming water and generating electricity. There are fuel cells of different types; the main candidate to be used in automobiles is the one based on the proton exchange membrane (also called solid polymer electrolyte fuel cell), due to its lower cost, adequate size, simple design, and operation at low temperatures.

Fuel-cell batteries require hydrogen, which may be generated in the automobile itself from ethanol, methanol, or natural gas.

Fuel cells are much more efficient than internal combustion engines and, as the fuel is electrochemically converted, they do not emit pollutant gases. Widely used in the United States space program, their high cost and size, until recently, hindered their use in automobiles. Important innovations achieved in the last 10 years have been changing this situation, making the cells one of the most promising technologies for the near future.

How much progress is being made in battery storage?

In 1859, the French physicist Gaston Planté invented the first lead-acid battery using two sheets of metal separated by a piece of linen and suspended in a glass jar of a sulfuric acid solution. Batteries widely used today are essentially variations of Planté's old invention.

The greatest advance in battery design since Planté occurred in the United States in 1977. Exxon developed and commercialized the lithium-ion battery, which consists of two electrodes separated by an electrolyte, often a polymer gel. When the battery is being charged, lithium ions migrate from the positive electrode, which is made from a lithium-based material, through the electrolyte to the negative electrode, which is usually made of carbon. When it is discharging, the ions flow in an external circuit attached to the battery. The positive electrodes are often made from lithium iron phosphate.

Lithium-ion rechargeable batteries became the most important storage technology in portable applications in recent years. They have a 90–95% efficiency, and their energy density is superior to all other commercial rechargeable batteries, being in the capacity range of 250–350 watt-hour/liter (100–200 watt-hour/kilogram). Lead-acid batteries have a capacity of 50–100 watt-hour/liter (5 to 50 watt-hour/kilogram).

Lithium-ion batteries come usually in 6.2 kilowatt-hour modules, which can be fitted together for several megawatt-hours of electricity. Some of the present electric cases on the market operate at 24 kilowatt-hours. These modules can be charged in as few as 30 minutes.

The properties of nickel-cadmium and nickel-metal hydride batteries lie between lead-acid and lithium-ion batteries.

What is the role of energy storage?

Renewable energies such as wind and solar are only intermittently available, so it is necessary to have a means to store the electricity that they generate.

Among the many energy-storage technologies available, pumped hydro has the highest rated power (around 1,000 MW) and discharge time (100 hours). Compressed air energy storage (CAES) comes next with 1–100 MW and a discharge time of 1–10 hours. Lithium-ion and a number of other batteries have a rated power between 0.01 and 1 MW and discharge times of 0.1–10 hours.

The most commonly used storage technology is compressed air energy storage (CAES). Progress has been made recently using adiabatic CAES in which the heat generated during compression can be stored and used again during decompression, considerably improving the efficiency of the system. For load leveling, compressed air stored in large underground salt caverns appears to be an economical and technically feasible option. Cost for long term storage with hydrogen are low due to its very high energy density.

Hydro systems are the most economical option, but because of geographic conditions and public acceptance, there is a limited potential for pumped hydro power plants.

What is the role of long-distance electricity transmission?

Transmission of electricity allows the pooling of different renewable energy sources, even on a transcontinental level, and can link areas with large renewable energy resources to regions with high electricity demand. While conventional alternating current transmission technology is not suited to transmitting electricity across distances of more than 500 km, High Voltage Direct Current (HVDC) technology can be used to link, for example, the vast solar resources in the world's Sun Belt to demand centers, thus facilitating the provision of dispatchable solar bulk electricity.

A number of companies are seriously considering covering large areas of the Sahara Desert with photoelectric cells and transmitting the electricity via HVDC thousands of kilometers to Europe. Transference of electricity over such large distances is not unusual.

One of the advantages of HVDC is the low cost for transmission of very high power over very long distances, in the range of 0.5–1.5 €ct/kWh. Losses incurred in transmitting power over a distance of 1,000 km total around 3%. Today's HVDC schemes have a maximum power of 3,000 MW and transmission distances of around 1,000 km. A new type of converter, called HVDC Light, was introduced in the late 1990s. Unlike AC cables, there is no physical restriction limiting the distance or power level for HVDC cables underground or under water. There is an emerging market for this new technology in transferring power under the sea, for example, from wind parks, to strengthen the electricity grid in areas where there are no overhead lines.

What are smart grids?

Smart grids consist of an intelligent monitoring system that keeps track of all electricity flowing in a system. They are capable of integrating intermittent renewable sources, such as solar and wind, and turning on home appliances, such as washing machines or other electric equipment.

The power grids of the 20th century were only capable of sending electricity from a few power stations to a large number of users. It was a unidirectional system. Smart grids are bidirectional and can accept and reroute electricity to and from many decentralized sources, including homes that have solar panels on their roofs. During the day, when the sun is shining, the homes can send energy to the grid and in the evenings (or when clouds block sunlight) the grid returns electricity to the homes, enabling net metering of the electricity consumed.

Smart grids capable of wireless network communication can also replace manual electricity meters.

What are the prospects of biomass?

The conversion of sunlight into chemical energy supports nearly all plant and animal life on Earth. It is estimated that 20 billion tons of carbon are stored per year by photosynthesis in terrestrial plants and another 13 billion dry tons in oceanic plants. Biomass is one of humanity's oldest energy resources, and it still accounts for approximately 10% of global primary energy consumption today. As much as one-third of the world's population relies on fuel wood, agricultural residues, animal dung, and other domestic wastes to meet household energy needs. Such traditional uses of biomass are estimated to account for more than 60% of the biomass contribution to global energy supply, most of which occurs outside the formal market economy and predominately in developing countries. Modern uses of biomass to generate electricity and heat or as a source of fuels for transportation are estimated to account for less than 40% of total biomass energy consumption worldwide.

Modern uses of biomass, however, offer a far greater array of possibilities for reducing dependence on fossil fuels, curbing greenhouse gas emissions, and promoting sustainable economic development. A range of biomass energy technologies, suitable for small- and large-scale applications, are available. They include gasification, combined heat and power (cogeneration) schemes, landfill gas, energy recovery from municipal solid wastes, or biofuels for the transportation sector (ethanol and biodiesel). Recent interest in biomass energy has focused primarily on applications that produce liquid fuels for the transportation sector. Given growing concerns about global petroleum supply and the current lack of diversity in available fuel options for the transport sector, such fuels represent the highest-value use of biomass energy at present. Ultimately, the most promising biomass applications of all are likely to involve integrated systems where, for example, biomass is used as both fuel and feedstock in the coproduction of liquid transportation fuels and electricity.

Is ethanol a good substitute for gasoline?

Ethanol (C_2H_6O) is a fuel used mainly in Otto-cycle engines, as a replacement for gasoline. As opposed to methanol, which is toxic and obtained from coal and other fossil sources, bioethanol is a very clean and renewable fuel. The traditional route used to produce ethanol is through sugar fermentation processes and distillation. This route is usually named first-generation technology. Ethanol can also be obtained from fossil sources by more sophisticated processes (such as the Fischer–Tropsch process, a set of chemical reactions that convert a mixture of carbon monoxide and hydrogen into liquid hydrocarbons) or acid or enzymatic hydrolysis of cellulosic materials, which are considered second-generation technology. The local benefits of using bioethanol as a fuel are evident in the city of São Paulo, Brazil, where widespread use of ethanol has reduced emissions of lead, sulfur, carbon monoxide, and particulate matter, significantly improving air quality. In addition, the use of ethanol provides global benefits in the form of reduced CO_2 emissions. Presently ethanol replaces approximately 50% of the gasoline that would be otherwise used in Brazil.

The Brazilian government encouraged the production of ethanol from sugarcane and the adaption of Otto-cycle engines to work with "pure" ethanol (hydrated alcohol with 96% ethanol and 4% water) or gasohol (a blend of 78% gasoline and 22% anhydrous ethanol). These two types of dedicated engines were recently replaced by flex-fuel vehicles (FFVs). By means of electronic sensors, FFV technology identifies which gasoline–ethanol blend goes through the vehicle injection system and adjusts the combustion conditions. With the flex vehicle, consumers have full freedom of choice, mainly determined by the price at the pump. Recent advances have made the flex technology relatively cheap (amounting to an additional cost of US$100 or less per automobile), with emissions close to or lower than those of gasoline. Today more than 95% of cars sold in Brazil are flex-fuel vehicles.

What are the prospects of biodiesel?

In 1912, Rudolf Diesel, stated that "the use of vegetable oils for engine fuels may seem insignificant today, but such oils may become, in the course of time, as important as petroleum and the coal-tar products of the present time."

Biodiesel production is based on trans-esterification of vegetable oils and fats through the addition of methanol (or other alcohols) and a catalyst. Glycerol is a co-product of the process. The characteristics of biodiesel fuels vary significantly depending upon the production technology and feed-stock used.

Biodiesel is a diesel replacement fuel that can be used in compression-ignition engines, and it is produced from renewable, non-petroleum-based sources such as vegetable oils (soy, mustard, castor, canola, rapeseed, and palm oils), animal fats (poultry offal, tallow, fish oils), and used cooking oils and fat grease (from restaurants and industries). The production of biodiesel from non-food feedstock is gaining special interest. In the United States and European Union, algae-based biodiesel promises very high yields per area— 15 times more than palm oil, 60 times that of rapeseed, and 200 times that of soybeans.

Biodiesel production depends on feedstock and land availability even more than bioethanol production. Although biodiesel is considered a "renewable" fuel, one of the materials needed for its production is methanol produced from natural gas, which is a fossil fuel. Advanced processes include the replacement of methanol of fossil origin by Fischer–Tropsch technology.

Biodiesel is also usually considered "sulfur-free," which is the case unless the biofuel is produced by catalysis with sulfuric acid. Biofuels are hygroscopic and easily biodegradable, which may be an environmental advantage, but also a quality-control problem, mainly when stored in hot and humid places. Overall, biodiesel combustion produces fewer pollutants than conventional fossil fuels, except for NO_x.

In Indonesia and Malaysia, palm oil biodiesel has been heavily criticized as being responsible for the clearance of native rainforests, with consequent biodiversity losses and land-use change, in addition to greenhouse gas emissions. These criticisms seem to have been exaggerated because less than 10% of the palm oil produced today is used for the production of biodiesel.

Is there competition between bioenergy and food?

The rise in the prices of agricultural products between 2007 and 2008, after several decades of declining real prices, is often seen as a cause of famine, and it has led to the politically laden controversy of fuel "versus" food.

Arguments have been made that the competition between land for fuel (namely ethanol) and land for food, in both the United States and Europe, is one of the causes of famine around the world and leads indirectly to deforestation in the Amazon and other tropical areas. In the aggregate, grain prices have more than doubled since January 2006, with over 60% of the rise occurring since January 2008, closely following the price of petroleum. More recently, however, the price of agricultural products has decreased following the decline in petroleum prices. In contrast, the point has been made that higher crop prices will not necessarily harm the poorest people; many of the world's 800 million undernourished people are farmers or farm laborers, who could benefit from higher crop prices.

To keep the issue in perspective, it is important to remember that, around the world, 93 million hectares are currently being used to grow soybeans and 148 million hectares for corn. In Brazil, bioethanol is mainly produced from sugar cane, over 5 million hectares of land, and in the United States, the largest producer of bioethanol in the world today, it is produced from corn, over 11 million hectares of land. In Europe, ethanol is mainly produced from sugar beets and wheat. China, the third largest world producer, produces ethanol from corn and wheat.

Worldwide, 1.5 billion hectares of the arable land is already being used for agriculture and another 440 million hectares is potentially available, including 250 million hectares in Latin America and 180 million in Africa. The area currently being used for biofuels is less than 1% of the land in use; even if this amount were to grow by an order of magnitude, it would not be a very disturbing expansion. This problem has been extensively analyzed in many reports, particularly by the World Bank, which pointed out that several individual factors have driven up grain prices and not biofuels production. Among them are high energy and fertilizer prices, the continuing depreciation of the US dollar, drought in Australia, growing global demand for grains (particularly in China), changes in some nations' import–export policies, speculative activity on future commodities trading, and regional problems driven by subsidies of biofuels production in the United States and Europe. Biofuel production does not seem to have been a particularly important driver of the 2008 surge in the price of cereals.

It has also been argued that deforestation in Amazonia can be attributed, directly or indirectly, to biofuels production in the southeast of Brazil. This is clearly incorrect: historical rates of deforestation in Amazonia are 0.5 to 1 million hectares per year and have been decreasing despite the expansion of sugarcane plantations in the southeast region of Brazil. In reality, deforestation in Amazonia is due to complex causes, the main ones being expansion of cattle raising and soya bean production, both unrelated to sugarcane expansion.

12

POLICIES

What are policy targets for renewable energy?

By early 2010, policy targets for the introduction of renewable energy at the national level existed in at least 85 countries worldwide, including all 27 European Union member states. In addition, many national targets for shares of electricity production from renewable energies range from 2 to 30%. Other targets exist for shares of total primary or final energy supply, specific installed capacities of various technologies, or total amounts of energy production from renewables, including heat. Targets also exist for biofuels in many countries.

The European Union aims to have 20% of its gross final consumption of energy and 10% of each member state's transport energy come from renewable sources by 2020.

What are biofuels mandates?

By 2010, 31 countries adopted biofuels mandates for ethanol (mixed in gasoline) and biodiesel (mixed in diesel oil). For ethanol these mandates usually range between 10 and 25%; for biodiesel they range between 2 and 10%, usually to be met before 2022 or earlier.

Brazil presently has an E-25 mandate in effect for ethanol, which means that a blend of 25% of ethanol and 75% regular gasoline is used throughout the country. In addition to that it has a B5 mandate for biodiesel meaning that a blend of 5% of biodiesel and 95% of regular diesel oil will be in use in 2013.

By 2010, 30 other countries (Argentina, Australia, Belgium, Bolivia, Canada, China, Colombia, Costa Rica, Czech Republic, Dominican Republic, Ethiopia, Finland, Germany, India, Italy, Malaysia, Netherlands, Norway, Pakistan, Panama, Paraguay, Peru, Philippines, Portugal, South Korea, Spain, Thailand, Uruguay, United Kingdom, and the United States) adopted mandates for ethanol, biodiesel, or both.

If one adds the amount of ethanol needed to meet the ethanol mandates up to 2022, one gets approximately 200 billion liters per year. Present production based first generation is around 70 billion liters (mainly in the United States and Brazil) per year, which replaces approximately 5% of the world's gasoline consumption at 1.2 trillion liters per year.

What are Renewable Portfolio Standards?

A renewable portfolio standard (RPS) is a government policy requiring that a minimum percentage of energy generation sold or capacity installed be provided by renewable energy. Public or private utilities are mandated to implement these targets.

RPS policies, also called renewable obligations or quota policies, exist at the state/provincial level in the United States, Canada, and India, and at the national level in Australia, South Korea, Chile, China, Italy, Japan, the Philippines, Poland, Romania, Sweden, and the United Kingdom. Globally, 63 states, provinces, or countries in 2010 had RPS policies. Most RPS policies require renewable power shares in the range of 5–20% by 2010 or 2012, although more recent policies are extending targets to 2015, 2020, and 2025. Most RPS targets translate into large expected future investments, although the specific means (and effectiveness) of achieving quotas can vary greatly among countries or states.

What are CAFE standards?

Fuel economy standards have been very effective in promoting engine efficiency and reduction in fuel consumption. The overall effectiveness of standards can be significantly enhanced if combined with fiscal incentives and consumer information.

The best example of such standards is the Corporate Average Final Economy (CAFE) standard, first introduced in the United States in 1975. Such standards set the average fuel consumption for the fleet of passenger car models and light trucks (with a gross vehicle weight rating of 3.866 kilograms or less) of each manufacturer.

The CAFE standard adopted originally was 25 miles per gallon (mpg). Subsequently, the European Union adopted a standard of 40 mpg. If the average fuel economy of a fleet from a given manufacturer falls behind the defined standard, that manufacturer must pay a penalty of US$5.50 per 0.1 mile per gallon under the standard, multiplied by the manufacturer's total production for the domestic US market. Since 1983, manufacturers have paid more then US$590 million in CAFE civil penalties to the US Treasury. Most European manufacturers regularly pay CAFE civil penalties ranging from less then US$1 million to more than US$20 million annually. Asian manufacturers and most of the big domestic manufacturers have never paid civil penalties.

In 2009 the US government proposed a new national fuel economy program for models 2012 to 2016, which ultimately requires an average fuel economy standard of 35.5 miles per gallon (39 mpg for cars and 30 mpg for trucks).

In 2011 an agreement was reached by the US government and the major automakers to increase fuel economy to 54.4 mpg for cars and light duty trucks by 2025.

What are "feed-in tariffs"?

"Feed-in tariffs" are a policy adopted at the state or national level but not at the international level, and they guarantee grid access to renewable energy producers and set a fixed guaranteed price at which power producers can sell renewable power into the electric power network.

Some policies provide a fixed tariff while others provide fixed premiums added to market or cost-related tariffs. By 2010, some 87 countries had adopted "feed-in" policies. The United States adopted them as early in 1970 and, in 1990, Germany followed. A number of other European countries adopted them over the subsequent decade. After the turn of the century many developing countries, along with states/ provinces in other countries, including Australia and Canada, adopted the same policy.

A "feed-in tariff" that provides a strong predictable stable price for renewable electricity has proved successful in some wealthy countries such as Germany and has accelerated investment in renewables. Setting quotas for renewable energy could be equally effective if the contracting process were to provide winning bidders with enough assurance that they could get financing at reasonable rates.

What is the Climate Convention?

The Climate Convention UNFCCC (United Nations Framework Convention on Climate Change) adopted in Rio de Janeiro, Brazil, during the Earth Summit in 1992 has as its ultimate objective the stabilization of the atmospheric concentrations of greenhouse gases at levels considered safe and achievable in a time frame compatible with the ecosystem's capacity of recovery and natural adaptation.

One of the basic principles of the Convention is that of "common but differentiated responsibilities," by which developed countries (Annex I countries) commit themselves to adopt national policies and limit anthropogenic emissions of greenhouse gases. In addition to that, they shall assist the developing countries (Annex II countries) that are particularly vulnerable to the adverse effects of climate change in meeting costs of adaptation to these adverse effects.

The Climate Convention has been in force since March 21, 1994. Today more than 190 countries have ratified it as "Parties to the Convention."

What is the Kyoto Protocol?

In 1997 the Conference of the Parties of the Climate Convention met in Kyoto, Japan and adopted the Kyoto Protocol, by which the Annex I countries (the industrialized countries) committed themselves to quantitative individual emission reduction targets to be reached in the period 2008–2012. Targets vary somewhat from country to country, but jointly they agreed to reduce emissions of the major greenhouse gases by at least 5% over 1990 levels. Developing countries (non-Annex I countries) were exempted from mandatory targets and time tables. For that reason the United States has signed but not ratified the Kyoto Protocol. Despite that, the Kyoto Protocol entered into force in 2005.

In order to reduce the emission mitigation costs, the Kyoto Protocol established three mechanisms:

1. Joint Implementation (JI),
2. Emission Trade (ET), and the
3. Clean Development Mechanism (CDM).

While JI and ET are mechanisms involving only industrialized countries, CDM involves developing countries as well.

According to the rules adopted by the Kyoto Protocol, for the CDM, Annex I countries can use certified emissions reduction from projects conducted in developing countries as part of their overall emission reduction commitments.

The reduction in emissions certified under CDM has to be additional to any that would occur in the absence of the certified project activity. For example, eliminating flaring of natural gas (methane) from oil exploration in developing countries and converting it into CO_2 would qualify because methane contributes more to climate warming than does CO_2. Afforestation in developing countries would also qualify.

The 2009 Copenhagen meeting of the parties of the Climate Convention saw a step backward in environmental governance. No decision was taken to extend the Kyoto Protocol beyond 2012, and the Protocol's mandatory commitments were replaced by voluntary pledges that in practice equalize actions by Annex I and non-Annex I countries. However, industrialized countries announced the establishment of a new fund to be administered by the Conference of the Parties for adaptation and to help developing countries implement measures to reduce their emissions. The fund should reach a value of $US100 billion per year in 2020.

A new effort was made at the Cancun Conference of the Parties in 2010 to extend the Kyoto Protocol beyond 2012, but it did not succeed. It did, however, take steps to operationalize the fund proposed in Copenhagen. The Conference recognized avoided deforestation as a valid instrument for the prevention of climate change and to reduce deforestation that contributes approximately 18% to the global CO_2 emission. The Conference decided that developing countries with tropical forests that succeed in reducing deforestation (and resulting CO_2 emissions) could receive international compensation for the avoided emissions. Such a mechanism is similar to CDM and is called REDD (Reducing Emissions from Deforestation and Forest Degradation). Norway has contributed US$100 million for REDD projects in Brazil.

In Durban, South Africa, in 2011 a second commitment period of the Kyoto Protocol was adopted while a new Protocol is negotiated. It was agreed that such negotiations will be concluded by 2015 to enter into force in 2020 establishing mandatory emission reductions for all countries.

What is "cap and trade"?

Cap and trade is a policy tool used to promote reductions in the amount of pollutants emitted by countries. It was originally used in the United States to reduce SO_2 emissions, which is the main contributor to acid rain. The policy operates in the following way: an overall mandatory cap is set by government on the amount of emissions that can be tolerated, and the industries responsible for the emissions receive quotas they cannot exceed. There is flexibility as to how to achieve these quotas, as industries might make changes to their production process or trade credits with other industries, since it is easier for some of them than for others to meet their allocated reductions. It has been a very successful program and promotes innovations and efficiency.

The European Union as a whole under the Kyoto Protocol is committed to an 8% reduction of greenhouse gas emissions, relative to 1990 figures, by 2012. The responsibility for meeting this commitment is shared among members states, based on agreed national allocations that are then transmitted to the leading emitters. Accordingly, the EUETS (European Union Emissions Trading System) was created to actively trade emissions. The price per ton of CO_2 equivalent emitted was set by the market, reaching 30 euros in 2006. But it fell to less than 5 euros in 2007, owing to an oversupply of emission permits.

The "cap and trade" scheme has the advantage of determining precisely by how many tons of CO_2 equivalent emissions need to be reduced, but the market determines the price of each ton.

What are carbon taxes?

Carbon taxes are another policy tool used to reduce CO_2 emissions, and they are levied on fossil fuels (coal, oil, and gas) according to their carbon content. Noncarbon sources of energy such as renewables and nuclear are not levied, which increases their competitive advantage. One advantage of carbon taxes over cap and trade is that they set a fixed cost to each ton of CO_2 equivalent, but the reductions that result from such taxes cannot be predicted with any degree of confidence.

The revenues generated by carbon taxes could also be achieved by auctioning permits in cap and trade. Cap and trade will be difficult to apply at a global level, but the process could start with subsets of countries administering cap and trade (as Europe has done) and eventually linking systems. Or there could even be parallel systems of cap and trade in some jurisdictions with carbon taxes in others.

Greenhouse gas pricing policies could be key in shifting energy systems toward low-carbon-emission technologies, fuels, and activities. While there is disagreement as to which pricing method is best—carbon taxes or cap and trade—the two approaches can be designed so that they are quite similar. Participants in cap and trade can approximate the price certainty of a carbon tax by setting price floors and ceilings for the cost of permits. To avoid severe impacts from human-caused climate change, wealthy countries must set the direct price or implicit price (resulting from regulations) for greenhouse gas emissions at least US$100 per tonne of CO_2 equivalent by 2020 and perhaps at well above US$300 by 2050. Developing countries must be protected from the full economic and equity impacts of such prices through transfers from wealthy countries. These transfers can be focused on the development of infrastructure necessary for the transition to a low-emission-energy system, including electric grids, low-emission generators, urban transit, and so on.

What is technological "leapfrogging"?

Because of the rapid growth of their energy consumption, developing countries are important theaters for innovation, especially in the energy-intensive basic materials industries (steel, chemicals, cement, etc.) for which demand has almost reached saturation in the industrialized countries. It is for this reason that it is so important that modern technologies be incorporated early into the process of development by "leapfrogging" the traditional path of development.

This process is already taking place, as demonstrated by the amazing speed of adoption and diffusion of innovative and state-of-the-art technologies in developing countries. A shining example is the speed at which cellular telephones were introduced even in countries that did not have traditional telephone systems, particularly in rural areas. Another example can be seen in Indian villages where lighting is provided by fluorescent lamps instead of old inefficient incandescent light bulbs. Other less spectacular technologies, such as biogas produced in large biogas units using waste products of the village, can serve several purposes such as power for lighting, water pumping, fertilizer production, and sewage treatment. Black-and-white television is becoming a thing of the past even in the remote areas of Amazonia. The same has happened with cellular telephones that have surpassed wire-connected telephones in many places.

Despite its attractiveness, "leapfrogging" should not be regarded as a universal strategy because sometimes the products or technologies needed are not available in developed countries or are not well suited to the developing country's needs. There is also usually a need to strike a balance between relative prices of labor and capital in developing countries. Because labor is expensive and capital is relatively cheap in industrialized countries, many innovative technologies produced in developing countries are labor-saving and capital-intensive. On the other hand, since labor is cheap and capital scarce the technologies adopted might be different. Developing countries need sometimes innovations better suited to their natural resource endowments than those they can obtain from industrialized countries. For example, not only is the production of biomass labor-intensive, it is also more readily available than fossil fuels in most tropical countries, including India, Brazil, and Indonesia. Hence, it is a major source of energy in many developing countries, but not necessarily in industrialized countries.

What is sustainable development?

The world's present energy system—heavily dependent on exhaustible fossil energy source—is not sustainable. In other words, it cannot last indefinitely.

The concept of sustainable development was proposed in the 1987 Brundtland Report, prepared at the request of the United Nations, in the following terms:

> Sustainable development is development that meets the needs of the present without compromising the ability of future generations to meet their own needs. It contains within it two key concepts:
> - the concept of "needs," in particular the essential needs of the world's poor, to which overriding priority should be given; and
> - the idea that technology and social organization can limit the environment's ability to meet present and future needs.

Looking at sustainable development in terms of energy can help to clarify the preceding definition, because the nature of the energy system offers a response to the thorny question of how many "future generations" we should consider.

As we have shown, fossil fuels are exhaustible, and, at constant production and consumption rates, the presently known reserves of oil will last around 41 years; natural gas will last for 64 years; and coal will last for 155 years. Owing to the dominance of fossil fuels in the world's energy supply and their expected limited lifetimes, they cannot be considered the world's main source of energy for more than one or two generations—thus providing a metric to the aim of "not compromising the ability of future generations to meet their own needs." Only renewable energy sources (and maybe nuclear energy if the other problems associated with its use could be solved) could do it.

From this perspective one should consider "sustainable development" as a "development that lasts."

PART V

NONTECHNICAL SOLUTIONS

13

ENERGY AND LIFESTYLE

What is the relationship between energy and lifestyles?

Broadly speaking, lifestyle is a pattern of daily living that is a combination of values, attitudes, interpretations, preferences, actions, and interactions in a particular time and space. Lifestyle choices are configured by multiple forces: technical, economic, political, institutional, and cultural. More succinctly, one could say that lifestyle is the way a person lives.

It is easy to describe rather than define lifestyle. Often lifestyle is described by diet type, individual wants and needs, world view, expenditure pattern, religion, geographic location, consumption level and pattern, leisure and work, and so on.

Consumption patterns and *lifestyle* are often assumed to be synonymous. The term lifestyle, as used by social scientists, refers to values, that is, social preferences, and there is a difference in degree between them: a great many behavioral changes (changes in consumption patterns) add up to value changes over time. A comparison can be made here between the evolution of lifestyles to the evolution of life itself: species evolve by adapting to a changing environment up to the point of becoming, in some cases, very different from the one from which they originated. In this sense, the introduction of the automobile could be compared with the great explosions in the evolution of life, such as that which took place in the Cambrian period, some 530 million years ago.

In the short run, incremental changes can be driven by consumers in a marketplace. And what people buy can be altered through information and education, to achieve a desired outcome. In the medium term, an approach that relies on human well-being in terms of sustainable development, on Millennium Development Goal (MDG) indicators, can have a moderate dampening effect on energy consumption.

The driving force of changing lifestyle could very well be technological development. The speed at which electricity, air transportation, and radio and television became basic and global ingredients of today's lifestyles points in that direction, despite cultural and social differences between and within countries.

However, it takes many behavioral alterations to change the scope of lifestyle or to incur new ones. For example, carpooling with neighbors to travel to work does not represent a change of lifestyle or in the way one values automobiles, but it could eventually lead to such changes.

If one looks specifically at energy consumption related to lifestyle changes, one can perceive that in the OECD countries, between 1975 and 2008, important changes occurred in the final uses of energy (see Table 13.1).

The amount of energy used by industry, which represented 32% of consumption in 1975, was reduced to 23% by 2008.

Table 13.1 OECD final energy consumption shares (%)

	1975	2008
Industry	32	23
Transport	26	33
Residential	20	19
Services	10	13
Others	12	12

Table 13.2 Non-OECD final energy consumption shares (%)

	1975	2008
Industry	35	34
Transport	13	18
Residential	34	30
Services	6	5
Others	13	14

This decline was made up, however, during the same period by the transportation sector, by which energy consumption increased from 26% to 33%. Such shifts in energy consumptions are reflected in lifestyles of the more affluent part of the world population.

In non-OECD countries transportation has a smaller role, but the residential sector has greater importance (see Table 13.2).

Is technological development the only driving force for changing lifestyles?

The driving force of changing lifestyles is, in some cases, technological development. On the one hand, this mechanistic view glosses over cultural, religious, and educational differences, but on the other hand, it seems to be rather convincing in explaining the homogeneity of consumption patterns in many parts of the world.

There is a convergence between consumption patterns and economic systems, and literature shows that consumption patterns between developed and less developed countries are becoming more and more similar.

For example, this manifests itself clearly in the impact of electricity consumption, as seen in Table 13.3.

The share of electricity in energy consumption has grown significantly, from 8.8% in 1973 to 17.2% in 2008.

Table 13.3 World's final energy consumption shares (%)

	1973	2008
Oil	46.8	41.6
Gas	14.2	15.6
Coal/peat	14.6	9.8
Electricity	8.8	17.2
Combustibles, renewables, and waste	14.0	12.7
Others	1.6	3.1
Total	100.0	100.0

The growing importance of electricity in modern society results from the fact that, once produced, it can be transported easily over long distances and is readily used in a variety of homes and offices. In this way it differs from other sources of energy such as solid fuels (e.g., coal) or liquid fuels (such as oil). In addition, it can be converted with almost 100% efficiency to mechanical work.

A shortcoming of electricity is that it is frequently produced from fossil fuels, so it is produced from fuels that are expensive and highly pollutant. This is the reason why electricity production from renewable energy sources (wind, photovoltaics, and others) is presently receiving so much attention.

What is the impact of transportation modes on lifestyles?

Table 13.4 shows typical energy consumption for different modes of passenger transport in kWh per kilometer, per passenger kilometer.

Automobiles consume at least three times more energy per passenger than busses and short-distance trains.

It is clear, therefore, that imaginative approaches to urban planning and public transportation can accomplish a great

Table 13.4 **Energy consumptions for different transportation modes**

Transport mode	Average speed (km/hour)	Energy consumption (kWh/per km)
Train (short distance)	59–84	0.07–0.13
Train (long distance)	100	0.23–0.28
Train (high-speed)	160	0.07
Automobile	100	0.33–0.49
Bus	45	0.11–0.13
Aircraft	700	1.22–2.03

deal. As an example, in the United States, mass transport accounts for only 6% of all passenger travel, while in Germany it is over 15% and in Japan 47%.

Transporting freight by road consumes approximately 10 times more fuel than by rapid transportation.

What are the major determinants of lifestyle changes?

Lifestyles strongly influence consumption patterns, particularly energy consumption levels. Some major determinants of lifestyle changes are fertility preferences, eating habits, religion, and climate.

Throughout the 1990s, patterns in family size reflected a continued long-term trend of wanting smaller families. The decline in fertility rates is commonly associated with better socioeconomic conditions and high levels of education for women, and urban areas are drivers of this trend. But the trend is particularly pronounced in some areas, for example, in Bangladesh, where modest increases in socioeconomic development overlap with drastic declines in fertility rates.

Another major determinant of consumer demand is taste and preference, in addition to price, income, marketing, consumer knowledge, situation, and food preferences. Ample evidence has been provided that religion influences consumer attitude and behavior in general, and food purchasing decisions and eating habits in particular. In many societies, religion even plays one of the most influential roles in food choice. The impact of religion on food consumption depends on the religion itself and on the extent to which individuals follow the teachings of their religion. Several religions forbid certain foods, for instance, pork and non-ritually slaughtered meat in Judaism and Islam, or pork and beef in Hinduism and Buddhism. Christianity has no food taboos.

Climate influences the way houses are built or even the bathing routine, which, for example, is extremely important to the Japanese lifestyle but also very energy intensive. Norwegians heat most of the living area most of the time, while the Japanese traditionally heat only the spaces they occupy, while they are occupying them.

One way to capture the importance of lifestyles in energy consumption is to analyze the behavior of the energy intensity of a country or a number of countries. Detailed studies in the OECD countries indicate that a decline in energy intensity over time is due to two different factors:

1. The introduction of energy-efficient technologies in manufacturing, transportation, households, and services, which are responsible for 80% of the reduction in energy intensity; and

2. Structural changes in consumption patterns, which are essentially changes in lifestyles, which account for the remaining 20%.

Appendix 1

Table A.1 Decimal Prefixes

deca (da)	10^1	deci (d)	10^{-1}
hector (h)	10^2	centi (c)	10^{-2}
kilo (k)	10^3	milli (m)	10^{-3}
mega (M)	10^6	micro (µ)	10^{-6}
giga (G)	10^9	nano (n)	10^{-9}
tera (T)	10^{12}	pico (p)	10^{-12}
peta (P)	10^{15}	femto (f)	10^{-15}
exa (E)	10^{18}	atto (a)	10^{-18}

Appendix 2

Table A.2 Common Energy Unit Conversion Factors

To:	Terajoule (TJ)	Gigacalorie (Gcal)	Megaton oil (equiv) (Mtoe)	Million British thermal units (Mbtu)	Gigawatt-hour (GWh)
From:	Multiply by:				
TJ	1	238.8	2.388×10^{-5}	947.8	0.2778
Mtoe	4.1868×10^4	10^7	1	3.968×10^7	11,630
Mbtu	1.0551×10^{-3}	0.252	2.52×10^{-8}	1	2.931×10^{-4}
GWh	3.6	860	8.6×10^{-5}	3,412	1

Source: IEA figures. Additional conversion figures available at http://www.iea.org/stat.htm

GENERAL REFERENCES

Earl Cook, Man, Energy, Society, W. H. Freeman and CO, San Francisco, CA, 1976

GEA 2012 Global Energy Assessment: Towards a Sustainable Future, Cambridge University Press, UK and New York, USA and International Institute for Applied Systems Analysis (IIASA) Laxenburg, Austria.

José Goldemberg, B. T. Johansson, A. K. N. Reddy, R. H. Williams, (Williams,) Energy for a Sustainable World, Wiley Eastern Limited, New Delhi, 1988

José Goldemberg and Oswaldo Lucon, Energy, Environment and Development, 2nd ed., Earthscan Publications Ltd, London and Sterling, VA, 2010

InterAcademy Council, Lighting the Way: Toward a Sustainable Energy Future, October 2007

Burton Richter, Beyond Smoke and Mirrors, Cambridge University Press, Cambridge, UK, 2010

Phil O'Keefe, Geoff O'Brien, and Nicola Pearsall, The Future of Energy Use, 2nd ed., Earthscan Publications Ltd, London and Sterling, VA, 2010

Vaclav Smil, Energy in Nature and Society, The MIT Press, Cambridge, MA, 2008

World Energy Assessment: Energy and the Challenge of Sustainability, 2000. UNDP (United Nations Development Programme), New York, http://www.undp.org/seed/eap

Chapters 1 and 2

John Bongaarts, "Population Policy Options in the Developing World," Science 263, 771–776, 1994

BP Statistical Review of World Energy, June 2010, http://www.bp.com/statisticalreview

Arthur Brooks, Gross National Happiness, Basic Books, New York, 2008

King Hubbert, The Energy Resources of the Earth, Scientific American 60, 224, 1971

Jean M. Martin, L'intensité energetique de l'activité economique dans les pays industialsés. Economies et Societe's—Cahiers de l'Ismea 22 (4), avril, 1998

UNDP International Human Development Indicators, http://hdi.undp.org

World Energy Statistics and Balances, IEA, 2010, (database)

Chapters 3–6

2010 Survey of Energy Resources, World Energy Council OECD/IEA, Paris, France

S. F. Baldwin, Biomass Stoves: Engineering Design, Development and Dissemination, Volunteers in Technical Assistance, Arlington, VA, 1987

BP Statistical Review of World Energy, June 2010, http://www.bp.com/statisticalreview

Dams and Development: a New Framework for Decision-Making: The Report of the World Commission on Dams, Earthscan Publications Ltd, London and Sterling, VA, November, 2000, http://www.dams.org

José Goldemberg, "Ethanol for a Sustainable Energy Future,"—Science 315, 808–810, February, 2007

D. O. Hall and K. K. Rao, Photosynthesis, Cambridge University Press, New York, 1999

IAEA, The Future of Nuclear Power, MIT, Cambridge, MA, 2003 (updated in 2008)

REN21, Renewables Energy Policy Network for the 21st Century, Global Status Report, Paris), 2010 Paris: REN21 Secretariat

Chapters 7–9

Analysis of the Scope of Energy Subsidies and Suggestions for the G-20 Initiative—IEA, OPEC, OECD, World Bank Joint Report Prepared for Submissions to the G-20 Summit Meeting, Toronto (Canada), June 26–27, 2010

A. Cherp, "Energy and Security" in GEA 2012 Global Energy Assessment: Towards a Sustainable Future. Cambridge University

Press, UK and New York, USA and International Institute for Applied Systems Analysis (IIASA) Laxenburg, Austria

European Commission, External Costs: Research Results on Socio-Environmental Damages due to Electricity and Transport, Luxembourg, 2003, http://ec.europa.eu/research/energy/pdf/externeen.pdf

IPCC, http://www.ipcc.de

Martin Junginger, Wilfried van Sark, André Faiij, and Edward Elgar, Technological Learning in the Energy Sector, Edward Elgar Publishing Inc, Cheltenham, Glos, UK, 2010

M. Wackernagel and W. Rees, Our Eecological Footprint: Reducing Human Impact on the Earth, New Society Publishers, Gabriola Island, BC, 1996

The World Commission in Environment and Development, Our Common Future, Oxford University Press, New York, 1987

Chapters 10–12

Dams and Development: A New Framework for Decision-Making: The Report of the World Commission on Dams, Earthscan Publications Ltd, London and Sterling, VA, November, 2000, http://www.dams.org

José Goldemberg, The Brazilian Experience with Biofuels, Innovations 4, 4, pp. 91–107, 2009. http://mitpress.mit.edu/innovations/

José Goldemberg, Leapfrogging Technology" Encyclopedia of Global Environmental Change, (Vol. 4) 295–296, 2001

The Kyoto Protocol to the Climate Convention http://www.unfcc.de

Lorna A. Greeming, David L Greene, and Carmem Difiglio, Energy Efficiency and Consumption—The Rebound Effect—A Survey, Energy Policy 28, 389–401, 2000

REN21, Renewables Energy Policy Network for the 21st Century, Global Status Report, Paris), 2010

F. Trieb, and H. Müller-Steinhagen, Europe—Middle East—North Africa, Cooperation for Sustainable Electricity and Water, Sustainable Science, 2, 205–219, 2007

United Nations Framework Convention in Climate Change, The Convention on Climate Change, http://www.unfcc.de

World Business Council for Sustainable Development (WBCSD), Energy Efficiency in Buildings Transforming the Market, 2009, http://www.wbcsd.org/DocRoot/WvNIJhLQBmCIKujoeNoh/91719_EEBReport_WEB.pdf

World Energy Outlook 2010 2010 International Energy Agency OECD/IEA Paris, France

Z. Zhaang, L. Lohr, Escalantec, M. Wetzstein, M. Food versus Fuel: What Do Prices Tell Us? Energy Policy 38, 445–451, 2010

Chapter 13

L. Nader and S. Beckerman, Energy as It Relates to the Quality and Style of Life, Annual Review of Energy 3, 1, 1978

INDEX